How Artificial Intelligence (AI)

Can Help

Genealogists

to Research, Organize, and Document

With Contrasting Examples

By

Lynn Zacny Busby

and "Aimy" (Chat GPT)

2505.01

ISBN: 9798329469257

Table of Contents

Introduction...4

Aimy and Me 5

AI Explained In Simple Terms 6

    What Is The Difference Between A Search Engine And AI 7

    What is the Difference Between Using AI And Understanding AI....................8

What is ChatGPT 8

What Is An AI "Prompt"...10

What Are Some Examples Of Well Worded Prompts To ChatGPT 10

What Are AI Hallucinations 11

How Does AI Get Smart? 11

How Smart Is Chatbot-3.5 12

Tips For New Users Of ChatGPT 13

What's The Best Way To Learn About AI and ChatGPT For A Beginner..............14

Deeper Dive - New Vocabulary Around AI 15

How Would A Genealogist Use ChatGPT...20

Specific Examples of Using AI To Improve Genealogy Research.........................21

Questions Answered?..22

    Why Would ANY English Gentlemen Go to Virginia in the 17th Century? 22

    Why Is It Difficult to Track Ancestorial Migration During 17th Century Virginia? 23

    Why Focus on Surnames and Social Class of Landowners?........................25

    Why Are Colonial Maiden Names So Illusive?...34

    Why Identify Events Occurring Around Similar Dates? 35

    Was There a French Connection in New Kent County Before 1700?...........36

    Why Would Any English Gentlemen Go to Virginia in the 17th Century? 38

    Why Is It Difficult to Track Ancestral Migration in 17th Century Virginia?........40

    Why Focus on Surnames and Social Class of Landowners? 43

    Why Identify the Amount of Acreage Owned? 46

    Why Find Specific Land Locations?...48

    Why Identify Neighbors of an Ancestor? 50

    Why Are Colonial Maiden Names So Elusive?..52

    Why Identify Events Around Similar Dates? 54

    Was There a French Connection in New Kent County Before 1700?...........57

Observations Comparing "The Book" Original Content And Aimy's Version: 59

Category PLACES - Geographic Overview of the Virginia Colony 59

Category EVENTS: Bacon's Rebellion 65

Category EVENTS - Timeline of Important Events in 17th Century Virginia 69

Category PEOPLE - 17th Century First Families of Virginia (FFV) 73

Category PEOPLE – Gideon Macon 79

Category METHODs: Discovering New Information In Old Data 98

AI for Genealogists as of July 2024..121

Can AI do graphics?...124

AI May Not Answer All Your Questions, But… 128

Details about the ChatGPT version used for this book:...131

Artificial Intelligence (AI) has been integrated into our lives for over a decade, often under the guise of an "assistant." These assistants subtly enhance our experiences by making automated suggestions tailored to our interests. For instance, Netflix recommends movies you might enjoy, Alexa provides the current temperature, Facebook displays ads based on your recent inquiries, Google answers your voice queries without requiring typing, and Ancestry.com offers hints about your family tree.

Recently, AI has become more prominent and accessible. Now, anyone with a computer can directly ask AI to generate text, receiving responses almost instantly. These responses are quick, spell-checked, grammatically correct, and punctuated correctly.

However, it's important to note that while AI always provides a response, it is not always factual. AI generates answers that may sound logical but can lack a basis in reality, a phenomenon known as "hallucination." Given this tendency, can AI still benefit genealogists who prioritize accuracy and the citation of original documents?

Despite its occasional inaccuracies, AI can be a valuable tool for genealogists. It can assist in organizing research, suggesting potential sources, and providing contextual information that might lead to further discoveries. The key is to use AI as a supplementary tool, verifying its suggestions with primary sources and documented evidence. This approach ensures that AI enhances genealogical research without compromising its integrity.

Background: I recently published a book on Amazon entitled

"Find the Living Truth in Dead Records," from now on, **referred to as "The Book"**

which delves into the intricate details of 17th-century Virginia through extensive research. Over many years, I diligently gathered data, noting its source, analyzing it, and making observations, aiming to inspire others to engage in similar research endeavors. "The Book" is a culmination of my efforts to present these findings in a coherent and accessible manner.

"The Book" has over 440 footnotes. During my journey, I relied heavily on Internet resources to unearth historical documents, accounting for approximately 98% of the data in the book.

However, following its publication, I delved deeper into artificial intelligence (AI) and realized its immense potential to enhance the research and writing processes. This newfound understanding led me to collaborate with AI, specifically an AI dedicated to language called ChatGPT, to see how it would "re-write" portions of my book.

Aimy is my nickname for "MY AI," formally known as ChatGPT-3.5.

Working with "Aimy," I compared AI-generated content to the content in "The Book," leveraging AI's ability to produce text with impeccable spelling, grammar, and punctuation. Aimy not only facilitated research but also contributed significantly to the writing process and would have resulted in a more refined and polished final product in a fraction of the time. The comparison between "The Book" and Aimy's version serves not only as a resource for genealogists, showcasing the use of AI in research and writing, but also as a testament to the remarkable quality and efficiency AI can bring to such endeavors.

To remove some of the mystery of AI, we (Aimy and I) present a brief tutorial about AI written by Aimy in response to the PROMPTs I gave her:

Note: The capitalized, bolded word "***PROMPT***" in the following text shows the exact wording I provided to Aimy, followed by her response, which is shown in *italics*. Given that AI is, by its nature, constantly improving, I also give the date of the response.

AI Explained In Simple Terms

PROMPT: in simple terms explain AI to a computer novice with examples of AI being commonly used today.

ChatGPT-3.5 as of 06/24/2024. (*Aimys' response in italics.*)

AI, or Artificial Intelligence, is like having a smart assistant on your computer or phone. It's a kind of technology that helps machines learn and make decisions like humans do. Here are some examples of AI that you might use every day:

1. ***Smart Assistants****: AI powers smart assistants like Siri, Alexa, or Google Assistant. They can answer questions, set reminders, play music, and even control smart home devices.*

2. ***Recommendation Systems****: Have you noticed how Netflix suggests movies you might like? That's AI at work, analyzing your watching habits to recommend shows and movies you might enjoy.*

3. ***Chatbots****: Many websites use chatbots to answer customer questions. These bots use AI to understand your queries and provide helpful responses.*

4. ***Social Media****: AI is used in social media platforms to show you posts and ads based on your interests and interactions.*

5. ***Autocorrect and Predictive Text****: When you type a message on your phone, AI helps autocorrect your spelling mistakes and suggests words or phrases you might want to use next.*

6. ***Online Shopping***: AI is used by online stores to recommend products based on your browsing history and shopping preferences.

7. ***Fraud Detection***: Banks and credit card companies use AI to detect unusual spending patterns and potential fraud, helping to keep your accounts safe.

These are just a few examples, but AI is becoming more and more common in our daily lives, making things easier and more efficient!

What Is The Difference Between A Search Engine And AI

PROMPT: What Is The Difference Between A Search Engine And AI

ChatGPT-3.5 as of 06/24/2024

Examples of search engines include Google, Bing, and Yahoo. They provide a list of relevant websites and resources based on your search query.

On the other hand, AI (Artificial Intelligence) refers to the ability of computers or machines to perform tasks that typically require human intelligence. This includes tasks like learning from experience, recognizing patterns, making decisions, and understanding natural language.

Here's how they differ:

1. ***Functionality***: *Search engines are designed to retrieve and present information based on specific queries. They don't learn or adapt over time. AI, on the other hand, can learn from data, improve its performance, and make decisions based on patterns and experiences.*

2. ***Complexity***: *Search engines use algorithms to match keywords with relevant content. AI systems are more complex and can handle tasks like language translation, image recognition, natural language processing (understanding and generating human language), and more.*

3. ***Examples***: *Google Search is a search engine that retrieves web pages based on your search terms. AI systems like chatbots (e.g., Siri, Alexa) can understand and*

respond to natural language, virtual assistants (e.g., Google Assistant), self-driving cars, recommendation systems, and more.

In summary, search engines help you find information online, while AI systems can perform a wide range of tasks that mimic human intelligence, from understanding language to making decisions.

What is the Difference Between Using AI And Understanding AI

PROMPT: what is the difference between using AI and understanding AI
ChatGPT-3.5 as of 06/24/2024

Using AI involves interacting with AI systems or applications to perform specific tasks or functions, such as generating text, analyzing data, or making predictions. It's about leveraging AI technology to achieve practical goals or solve problems efficiently.

On the other hand, understanding AI goes deeper into comprehending the underlying principles, algorithms, and techniques that power AI systems. It involves learning about machine learning algorithms, neural networks, natural language processing (NLP), computer vision, and other AI-related concepts.

In simpler terms, using AI is like driving a car—you're using it to get from point A to point B. Understanding AI is like knowing how the car's engine works, how to maintain it, and how it enables you to move forward.

So, using AI focuses on the practical application of AI technology, while understanding AI delves into the theoretical and technical aspects of how AI works.

What is ChatGPT

PROMPT: What is ChatGPT
ChatGPT-3.5 as of 06/24/2024

ChatGPT, also known as Chat with GPT, is an AI-powered conversational agent developed by OpenAI. It's based on the GPT (Generative Pre-trained Transformer) architecture, specifically GPT-3.5 in my case. This model is designed to understand and generate human-like text based on the input it receives.

ChatGPT can engage in conversations, answer questions, provide information on a wide range of topics, offer advice, generate creative content such as stories or poems, and much more. It's capable of understanding context, maintaining coherence in discussions, and adapting its responses based on the conversation's flow.

Users can interact with ChatGPT through text-based platforms like this one, where they input their queries or prompts, and the AI generates responses accordingly. It's often used for tasks like customer support, language translation, content generation, and educational purposes.

PROMPT: explain ChatGPT in simple terms to a computer novice and give examples
ChatGPT-3.5 as of 06/24/2024

Sure, I can simplify that! ChatGPT is like a really smart computer friend you can talk to. It's not a real person, but it's designed to understand what you're asking and give you helpful answers.

For example:

- *If you ask it about the weather, it can tell you the forecast.*
- *If you're curious about space, it can explain planets and stars.*
- *If you need help with math homework, it can solve equations for you.*
- *If you're bored, it can even tell you jokes or stories!*

It's kind of like having a virtual encyclopedia and a friendly chat buddy all in one!

PROMPT: What Is An AI "Prompt"

ChatGPT-3.5 as of 06/24/2024

An AI prompt is like a question or request you give to a smart computer program. You tell the program what you want to know or do, and it uses its knowledge and abilities to give you a response or take action based on what you asked. It's like giving instructions to a helpful digital assistant.

What Are Some Examples Of Well Worded Prompts To ChatGPT

PROMPT: Can you provide Some Examples of Well Worded Prompts To ChatGPT
ChatGPT-3.5 as of 06/24/202

Sure, here are some examples of well-worded prompts for ChatGPT:

1. *"Can you explain the concept of quantum entanglement in simple terms?"*
2. *"I'm looking for advice on starting a small business. What are the key steps I should take?"*
3. *"Could you provide a brief overview of the causes and effects of climate change?"*
4. *"I'm curious about the history of the Roman Empire. Can you summarize its rise and fall?"*
5. *"What are some effective strategies for improving mental health and well-being?"*
6. *"I need help troubleshooting a computer issue. How can I resolve frequent crashing?"*
7. *"What are the benefits and drawbacks of renewable energy sources compared to fossil fuels?"*
8. *"Can you recommend some classic novels that are must-reads for literature enthusiasts?"*
9. *"I'm interested in learning more about meditation techniques for beginners. Where should I start?"*
10. *"Could you explain the basics of blockchain technology and its applications?"*

These prompts are clear, specific, and cover a wide range of topics that ChatGPT can provide information and assistance on.

What Are AI Hallucinations

PROMPT: in simple terms what are AI hallucinations and how can I *about them to only use documented facts. *(*note the error in my original prompt, which is missing the word, know))*

ChatGPT-3.5 as of 06/24/2024

AI hallucinations are images or visual content created by artificial intelligence that don't represent reality accurately. They're like digital dreams, where AI generates images based on its understanding of data, sometimes resulting in surreal or unrealistic pictures.

To avoid AI hallucinations and stick to documented facts, you can:

1. *Use reliable AI models: Choose AI tools and models known for accuracy and reliability in generating content.*
2. *Verify sources: Double-check information and images generated by AI against trusted sources or data.*
3. *Understand limitations: Recognize that AI can make mistakes or create imaginative content not grounded in reality.*
4. *Cross-reference: Compare AI-generated content with existing knowledge or other sources to ensure accuracy.*
5. *Review results: Take time to review AI outputs critically, especially if they seem unusual or improbable.*

How Does AI Get Smart?

PROMPT: How Does AI Get Smart?

ChatGPT-3.5 as of 06/24/2024

AI gets "smart" through a process called machine learning. Here's a simplified explanation:

1. ***Data Collection:*** *AI systems are trained using large amounts of data. For example, to teach an AI about dogs, it needs to see lots of pictures and descriptions of dogs.*
2. ***Training:*** *Using this data, the AI learns patterns and relationships. It identifies features that distinguish dogs from other animals, like cats or birds.*
3. ***Algorithms:*** *AI uses algorithms (mathematical rules) to process the data and learn from it. These algorithms adjust based on the data they receive, becoming more accurate over time.*
4. ***Feedback Loop:*** *As the AI makes predictions or responses, it receives feedback. If it's correct, it reinforces that learning. If it's wrong, it adjusts its approach.*
5. ***Iterative Improvement:*** *Through repeated cycles of training, testing, and refining, AI systems improve their accuracy and performance. They become "smarter" by learning from their experiences and the data they process.*

This process allows AI to handle complex tasks like language translation, image recognition, and decision-making based on data.

How Smart Is Chatbot-3.5

PROMPT: How Smart Is Chatbot-3.5
ChatGPT-3.5 as of 06/24/2024

Chatbot-3.5, like any technology, is continuously improving. As of my last update in 2022, ChatGPT-4 is quite advanced compared to earlier versions. It can engage in more complex conversations, understand context better, and generate more accurate and human-like responses. However, its "smartness" can vary depending on the specific task or topic you're discussing. For general conversations, it can provide nuanced and relevant responses, but it may still have limitations in highly specialized or technical areas.

Tips For New Users Of ChatGPT

PROMPT: Tips For New Users Of ChatGPT

ChatGPT-3.5 as of 06/24/2024

To get good results from ChatGPT as a new user, here are some tips:

1. **Clear and Specific Queries:** Provide clear and specific queries or questions to ChatGPT. The more precise your input, the better the response will be.

2. **Contextual Information:** Include relevant context or background information when asking questions. This helps ChatGPT understand the context of your query and provide more accurate answers.

3. **Use Complete Sentences:** Frame your queries in complete sentences rather than using fragmented phrases. This helps ChatGPT understand the structure of your request better.

4. **Review and Edit:** After receiving a response from ChatGPT, review it carefully. If necessary, edit your query or provide additional information to refine the results.

5. **Patience and Iteration:** Sometimes, it may take a few exchanges to get the desired information. Be patient and iterate on your queries based on ChatGPT's responses.

6. **Utilize Prompts:** If you're unsure how to frame a question, you can use prompts or examples provided by ChatGPT to guide your query.

7. **Feedback:** Provide feedback on the responses you receive. If the answer is helpful, acknowledge it. If not, clarify or rephrase your question for better results.

By following these guidelines, you can improve the quality of interactions and get more accurate and relevant results from ChatGPT.

PROMPT: What's The Best Way To Learn About AI and ChatGPT For A Beginner

ChatGPT-3.5 as of 06/24/2024

For a beginner looking to learn about AI and ChatGPT, here's a step-by-step approach:

1. *Understand AI Basics:*
   - *Start by grasping the fundamental concepts of artificial intelligence, including machine learning, natural language processing (NLP), and neural networks. Online courses and tutorials can be helpful for this.*
   - *Learn about different types of AI, such as supervised learning, unsupervised learning, and reinforcement learning.*

2. *Introduction to ChatGPT:*
   - *Familiarize yourself with what ChatGPT is and how it works. Understand that it's a language model trained on a vast amount of text data to generate human-like responses.*
   - *Explore the capabilities of ChatGPT, such as answering questions, generating text, assisting in writing, and providing information on various topics.*

3. *Hands-On Practice:*
   - *Use interactive platforms or tools that allow you to interact with ChatGPT directly. This hands-on experience will help you understand how to formulate prompts and receive responses.*
   - *Experiment with different types of prompts and observe how ChatGPT responds. Start with simple prompts and gradually move on to more complex ones.*

4. *Learn About Prompting Techniques:*
   - *Dive deeper into the art of crafting effective prompts for ChatGPT. Understand how to structure prompts to get accurate and relevant responses.*

- o *Explore techniques such as fine-tuning prompts, using context, leveraging examples, and providing clear instructions.*

5. *Explore Use Cases:*

- o *Study real-world use cases where ChatGPT is being used effectively. This could include customer support chatbots, content generation, language translation, and more.*
- o *Analyze how ChatGPT is applied in different industries and domains, such as healthcare, education, marketing, and entertainment.*

6. *Join Communities and Forums:*

- o *Engage with AI and ChatGPT communities online. Participate in forums, discussion groups, and social media channels where AI enthusiasts share knowledge and experiences.*
- o *Ask questions, seek advice, and learn from the experiences of others who are working with AI technologies.*

7. *Continuous Learning:*

- o *AI is a rapidly evolving field, so stay updated with the latest advancements, research papers, and developments in ChatGPT and related AI models.*
- o *Follow reputable AI blogs, attend webinars, and explore online courses to deepen your understanding and skills in AI and ChatGPT.*

By following these steps and maintaining a curious and explorative mindset, you can gradually build a strong foundation in AI concepts and become proficient in using ChatGPT for various applications.

Deeper Dive - New Vocabulary Around AI

PROMPT: what are new vocabulary words used around AI, and provide simple definitions of these AI related technology

ChatGPT-3.5 as of 06/24/2024

Here are some new vocabulary words related to AI and their definitions in simple terms:

1. ***Artificial General Intelligence (AGI)***: *Artificial General Intelligence (AGI) is a type of AI that can understand, learn, and apply knowledge just like a human. Unlike today's AI, which is designed for specific tasks (like recognizing faces or playing chess), AGI would be able to perform any intellectual task that a human can do. It would have the ability to reason, solve problems, and understand complex ideas across a wide range of topics, adapting to new situations much like a person would.*

2. ***Machine Learning (ML)***: *Machine Learning (ML) is a way for computers to learn from experience. Instead of being explicitly programmed to perform a task, a machine learning system is fed data and uses this data to make predictions or decisions. Over time, it gets better at its tasks by learning from new data, similar to how humans improve their skills through practice.*

3. ***Deep Learning***: *Deep Learning is a type of machine learning that uses special computer programs called neural networks, which are inspired by the human brain. These networks have many layers of nodes (neurons) that process information. Each layer learns to recognize different features or patterns in the data. By using many layers, deep learning can understand very complex patterns and make accurate predictions or decisions, such as recognizing objects in photos or understanding speech.*

4. ***Neural Network***: *A Neural Network is a computer program designed to work like the human brain. It has many small units called neurons, which are organized in layers. Each neuron takes in information, processes it, and passes it on to the next layer of neurons. Through this layered process, a neural network can learn to recognize patterns, such as identifying a cat in a picture or translating languages.*

5. ***Natural Language Processing (NLP)***: *Natural Language Processing (NLP) is a type of artificial intelligence that allows computers to understand, interpret, and respond to human language. This means that with NLP, computers can read text, hear speech, understand it, and even talk back to us in a way that makes sense.*

It's used in things like chatbots, voice assistants (like Siri or Alexa), and translation services.

6. **Computer Vision**: Computer Vision is a type of artificial intelligence that enables computers to see and understand images and videos. It allows computers to recognize objects, people, and scenes, just like humans do. For example, with computer vision, a computer can identify faces in a photo, read handwritten text, or even drive a car by recognizing and interpreting road signs and other vehicles.

7. **Reinforcement Learning**: Reinforcement Learning is a type of machine learning where a computer learns to make decisions by trying different actions and learning from the results. Imagine a computer program that is like a robot playing a game. Each time the robot makes a move, it gets feedback—points for good moves and penalties for bad ones. Over time, the robot learns to make better decisions to get the most points. It's like training a pet with rewards and corrections.

8. **Generative Adversarial Networks (GANs)**: Generative Adversarial Networks (GANs) are a type of artificial intelligence system made up of two competing neural networks: a generator and a discriminator. The generator creates new data, like images or text, while the discriminator's job is to tell the difference between real data and the data generated by the generator. They work together in a kind of game—while the generator tries to create data that's realistic enough to fool the discriminator, the discriminator gets better at telling real from fake. This competition helps the generator improve, creating more and more realistic data. It's like a forger trying to make fake paintings that are so good, even art experts can't tell they're fake.**Transfer Learning**: A technique in machine learning where a model developed for a particular task is reused as the starting point for a model on a different but related task.

9. **Explainable AI (XAI)**: Explainable AI (XAI) is a way to make artificial intelligence systems more understandable and transparent to humans. It's like having a clear explanation for why a decision was made by an AI system. For example, if an AI

suggests a certain medical diagnosis, XAI would provide the reasons behind that suggestion, like which symptoms or data points led to that conclusion. This helps people trust and verify AI's decisions, especially in critical areas like healthcare or finance.

10. ***Supervised Learning****: Supervised Learning is a type of machine learning where the computer is taught with labeled data. Imagine you're teaching a computer to recognize different types of fruits. You show it pictures of apples, bananas, and oranges, and you tell the computer which fruit is which. The computer then learns to identify these fruits based on the features you've shown it. It's like teaching a child by giving them examples and telling them what each thing is called.*

11. ***Unsupervised Learning****: Unsupervised Learning is a type of machine learning where the computer learns from data that isn't labeled. Imagine you have a bunch of different fruits but you don't tell the computer what each one is. Instead, you let the computer group the fruits based on similarities it sees in the data. So, it might group all the apples together, all the bananas together, and all the oranges together without being told what they are. It's like organizing things based on how they look alike rather than knowing their names beforehand.*

12. ***Semi-Supervised Learning****: Semi-Supervised Learning is a mix of supervised and unsupervised learning. Imagine you're teaching a computer to sort fruit, but you only label some of the fruits—like apples and bananas—but not all of them. The computer uses the labeled examples to learn patterns and then applies that knowledge to sort the unlabeled fruits. It's like having a few examples of labeled fruits to start with, and then using that knowledge to figure out how to sort the rest of the fruits.*

13. ***Federated Learning****: Federated Learning is a way for multiple devices to work together to train a machine learning model without sharing their data directly. Imagine you have several friends studying for a test together. Each friend has different notes and knowledge. Instead of sharing all their notes, they each study independently and only share their summaries or insights with the group. In*

Federated Learning, devices like smartphones or computers learn from their local data and then share what they've learned with a central model, helping improve the overall AI without compromising privacy by sharing personal data.

14. ***Edge AI****: Edge AI refers to artificial intelligence algorithms and processes that occur locally on a device, such as a smartphone, rather than relying on a centralized server or cloud. It's like having a mini brain inside your phone that can make decisions and perform tasks without needing to constantly connect to the internet. This allows for faster responses, reduced latency, and better privacy because sensitive data doesn't always need to be sent to external servers for processing.*

15. ***Bias Mitigation*** *Bias mitigation in AI is about reducing unfairness or prejudice in the decisions made by AI systems. Imagine you're teaching a robot to identify fruits, but it keeps thinking all green fruits are apples. You'd need to correct this bias by showing it more examples of other green fruits like grapes or kiwis. In AI, bias mitigation involves adjusting algorithms and data to ensure that decisions are fair and unbiased, especially in areas like hiring, lending, or healthcare where biased decisions can have serious consequences.*

16. ***Quantum Computing****: Quantum computing is like having a super-powered computer that uses the principles of quantum mechanics to perform operations. In regular computers, information is processed in bits, which can be either a 0 or a 1. But in quantum computers, these bits, called qubits, can be both 0 and 1 at the same time, thanks to a property called superposition. This allows quantum computers to perform complex calculations much faster than classical computers, with potential applications in areas like cryptography, drug discovery, and optimization problems.*

17. ***Autonomous Systems****: Autonomous systems are like smart machines that can do tasks on their own without constant human control. Imagine a robot vacuum cleaner that can navigate your house, avoiding obstacles and cleaning efficiently without you having to guide it all the time. Autonomous systems can include self-*

driving cars, drones, and even factory robots that can work independently once they're set up and programmed. They use sensors, algorithms, and decision-making capabilities to operate safely and effectively without human intervention.

18. **Ethical AI**: Ethical AI is about making sure artificial intelligence systems are used in a fair and responsible way. It's like teaching AI to follow the rules of good behavior, just like we teach people. This means considering things like fairness, transparency, privacy, and the impact AI can have on society. For example, making sure AI doesn't discriminate against certain groups of people or that it protects people's private information. Ethical AI aims to ensure that AI benefits everyone and doesn't cause harm or unfairness.

19. **AI Governance**: AI governance is like creating rules and guidelines for how artificial intelligence should be used and managed. It's similar to how we have laws and regulations for things like driving or building houses. AI governance involves making decisions about who can use AI, how it should be used ethically, and what steps should be taken to ensure AI systems are safe and fair. It's about balancing the benefits of AI with the potential risks and making sure AI is developed and deployed responsibly for the benefit of society.

How Would A Genealogist Use ChatGPT

PROMPT: How Would A Genealogist Use ChatGPT?

ChatGPT-3.5 as of 06/24/2024

A genealogist could use ChatGPT in several ways:

1. *Research Assistance:* ChatGPT can help genealogists by providing information about historical records, family names, migration patterns, and cultural contexts. Genealogists can ask specific questions like "What were common surnames in 17th-century Virginia?" or "Where can I find records of land ownership in colonial America?"

2. *Storytelling and Documentation:* Genealogists can use ChatGPT to craft narratives or document family histories. They might ask for writing tips, prompts for storytelling, or guidance on organizing information effectively.

3. *Analysis and Interpretation:* ChatGPT can assist genealogists in analyzing complex data, deciphering historical documents, and interpreting findings. For example, they might ask for help in understanding old handwriting or deciphering abbreviations in historical records.

4. *Collaboration and Networking:* Genealogists can use ChatGPT to connect with other researchers, share insights, discuss challenges, and exchange ideas. They can ask for tips on networking within the genealogy community or finding online resources for collaboration.

5. *Educational Purposes:* Genealogists can use ChatGPT to learn new techniques, stay updated on genealogy trends, or explore advanced research methods. They might ask for recommendations on genealogy courses, books, or workshops.

Overall, ChatGPT can be a valuable tool for genealogists, providing support, information, and inspiration throughout their research journey.

Specific Examples of Using AI To Improve Genealogy Research

Comparing "The Book" to Aimy's responses

The next sections show examples of how AI produces useful results from a specific prompt and compare them to real genealogical research already done in "The Book."

PROMPT: as an expert genealogist and reporter, re-write the following to make it better:

(The original genealogical research in "The Book" is shown below in gray so the reader can see what a human author had written and compare it to Aimy's version.

"The Book" begins by asking and answering some general questions about genealogical research challenges regarding distant ancestors.

Questions Answered?

Genealogy is like putting together a giant jigsaw puzzle ... the more you complete, the easier it gets. However, throwing in some pieces from a different puzzle serves to confuse and diffuse effort.

Having spent years investigating the early colonization of Virginia and its history as it pertains to the DePriest family, I continue to find more information that fosters some logical conclusions and/or offers some plausible speculation about the period.

To research something in detail, it is necessary to limit focus. There is a plethora of interesting information available for the period but trying to cover everything that happened to all the people in Colonial New Kent, Virginia, in detail is simply too broad to comprehend in one book. In addition to the topics included, an effort has been made to edit out interesting content that is not directly related to the focus of this study.

Though the series of The DePriest Gang books dispelled several myths about DePriest ancestry, information regarding the progenitor, Robert DePriest of New Kent County, was relatively scant. A fundamental desire to know more and understand why this Frenchman decided to settle in the county of New Kent, Virginia, back in 1689 was the impetus of this book. In pursuit of the 'why,' it seemed essential to know more about the environment during 17th century Virginia and New Kent County.

Why Would ANY English Gentlemen Go to Virginia in the 17th Century?

Given the very harsh conditions of the early Virginia settlers from disease, starvation, weather, skirmishes with local Indians, lack of medical care, heavy work demands, and very high death rates in general, why would any Englishmen, much less the well-to-do gentlemen, be, willing to risk their life to go to Virginia?

Land of Second Sons and Opportunity

Primogeniture was the right, by law or custom, of the firstborn child to inherit the parent's **entire** or central estate in preference to shared inheritance among all or some children. The goal of primogeniture was to keep the legacy family estate solid and wealthy instead of cutting it up amongst siblings and thereby weakening the position of the family name.

Most Gentry early settlers in Virginia were so-called "Second Sons." The English custom of primogeniture favored first sons' inheriting the lands and titles in England. Second and Third sons were left to develop wealth on their own. Many of these "spare" sons of English Noblemen had shown loyalty to the King and, as such, were called Cavaliers who were rewarded with large land grants in Virginia. With Governor William Berkeley's help, these Gentlemen formed the Southern elite in Colonial America and established Virginia's culture. These "spare sons" were well educated and carried the prestige of their heritage surname but not the money associated with it.

Note: "Primogeniture" is Latin for "firstborn." It was a rule from feudal England carried over into English Common Law that the oldest son would inherit the entire land estate of his parents. In Virginia, it only applied to those who died without a will.

Why Is It Difficult to Track Ancestorial Migration During 17th Century Virginia?

Historians have observed that early Virginians moved more frequently than their New England counterparts. It was not uncommon to see up to 20% change in county inhabitants over one year. With high death rates and new immigrants, land changed ownership frequently. The general culture of Virginia seemed to subscribe to the belief that 'the grass is always greener.'

In early Virginia, counties often changed borders and names as the number of inhabitants increased. Changes that appear in documents were often due to the evolving partitioning of the colony rather than people physically moving to a different county. For example, the same land around Totopotomoy Creek started as part of St Peter's Parish of New Kent County. Later, the western section became part of St. Paul's Parish of the newly formed Hanover County.

Land registered in York County was later part of New Kent County, which was created from York in 1654. Likewise, land registered in northern New Kent County later became part of King William County in 1720.

Maps of the time are beneficial for seeing who lived adjacent to whom, but only the surnames of major players were included on maps as landmarks. The word "Quarter" was also used during the colonial period to indicate large plots of land leased out to others for tenant farming but not the primary residence of the owner.

The most straightforward map of the geographic area of New Kent for this book was created in 1770 by John Henry and Thomas Jefferys,[1] The pertinent area for the DePriests and their neighbors was located south of the Pamunkey River and north of the Chickahominy River between Totopotomoy Creek down to Matadequin Creek shown as the highlighted area shown on the Henry/Jefferys map below:

---

[1]"A new and accurate map of Virginia wherein most of the counties are laid down from actual surveys." Names Created / Published. London, Thos. Jefferys, 1770.
https://www.loc.gov/resource/g3880.ct000431/?r=0.593,0.42,0.147,0.063,0 Accessed 12/02/23.

Why Focus on Surnames and Social Class of Landowners?

It is interesting to remember that Jamestown, Virginia, started developing settlements thirteen years before the 1620 Plymouth Rock landing of the Pilgrims in Massachusetts and evolved much differently from New England economically and socially.

Historian David Hackett Fisher's classic book Albion's Seed is helpful in understanding the differing cultures of developing America. He found that the cultures of the various areas of the developing country had distinct differences in values, and settlers tended to stay within that cultural environment or take it with them when they moved. Thus, someone who landed in America in the aristocratic culture of Virginia was doubtful to have 17th-century relatives appear in New England even if they share the same surname.

Many of the surnames that started in Virginia have been carried forward throughout the South of the United States for many generations.[2]

The more unique a surname, the easier to track, but the more likely to encounter misspellings. Regarding the DePriest surname in America, it can be assumed that the earliest record of a DePriest in Virginia pointed to the progenitor of the family of American DePriest decedents. A surviving parish document shows a Robert DePross/DePrest *(DePriest)* on a list of 1689 New Kent County landowners. He is assumed to be the American Progenitor since the surname was the earliest mentioned in America, specifically in Virginia. It is doubtful that unusual surname would also be found in New England in the 17th century.

The King of England ordered the Colonial Virginia Parishes to perform "processionings" to delineate the borders of land ownership to know who owed how much in taxes. Cleaner property boundary definition was a side benefit. The surviving colonial Parish Vestry records of 17th century New Kent, Virginia, provide a list of landowners whose land was "processioned" approximately every four years. These processioning lists can be extremely helpful for a researcher to identify/verify changing neighbors and timelines in peoples' lives.

Note: The records of St. Peter's and St. Paul's parishes of New Kent County and neighboring Hanover County are the most complete surviving records of any parish in the 17th and early 18th centuries.

Migration within Virginia was common as settlers sought more opportunities, and the fertility of the land was an essential factor. Tobacco crops quickly used up the soil's

---

[2] Fischer, David Hackett, Albion's Seed : Four British Folkways in America. New York :Oxford University Press, 1989.

nutrients. The richest soil tended to be around the major rivers and was the most desirable, so it was settled first as new land areas were opened up for settlers.

Descriptions of land grants in colonial records often refer to natural landmarks to identify the location of land owned by various grantees of New Kent County (including its predecessor counties and other surrounding counties). Rivers and creeks were commonly used to help identify and specify an area. References to the Pamunkey and Chickahominy rivers are a great help in identifying neighbors, as well as references to the Totopotomoy and Matadequin creeks. All these water bodies also had many and various misspellings as they maintained the names given to them by the local native Americans. For clarity, I have corrected the many misspellings of these landmark bodies of water.

Church Parish records were divided into two categories: the parish register, which recorded birth, marriage, and death records. They are the best we have, yet they are incomplete, for it is known that births occurred but were not recorded and known death dates and marriage partners are often missing.

The parish's business was documented in the Parish Vestry records. They were an accounting of the business side of the parish: who was owed or paid for what and who was responsible for building infrastructure within a precinct, like roads and bridges. Also included were decisions about criminal punishments, welfare for disabled people, orphans, etc., and recorded changes in the parish's leaders and their rotating roles within the church.

The Gentry class is important to recognize as they represented the elite class of Virginians who "made the rules." They became the leaders of the colony of Virginia via parish roles and government leadership roles and typically did not mix socially with common yeoman (farmers). That fact can often help researchers eliminate some speculation about marriage partners. The culture dictated that a member of the gentry class would never marry into a yeoman family of little wealth because the goal of the Gentry class marriage was to maintain wealth within blood and marriage related family. A term used by Historian Fisher is that it was an "oligarchy of cousins." This fact negates the idea that the daughter from the super wealthy Bolling family would ever have married a mere yeoman DePriest in the 17th Century as some family trees would (*falsely*) indicate.

Much has been documented about the First Families of Virginia (FFV) and the Gentry class of landowners which can be helpful in making logical speculation. Most of the Gentry's land was obtained through land patents which included a description of the location of the property. Most landowners however were yeoman planters who mostly obtained their small farms outside of the government documented land patent system and documentation about the location of this land is often nonexistent. Thus, if a researcher can determine the closeness of a Yeoman Ancestor's land to land granted to a member of the Gentry via a formal patent, it is possible to get an idea of the location of a Yeoman's land not extant by a sale/transfer from the original grantee. The processioning documents are very helpful as they further divided the parish into precincts in which both Gentry and Yeoman were grouped.

Why Identify the Amount of Acreage Owned?

In Colonial Virginia, land ownership indicated wealth which in turn indicated social prestige and political power.

The rules of land ownership of the time required documenting government patents given to key individuals and/or earned via the headright system. Key individuals who earned the King's favor were rewarded with large land grants in Virginia as an enticement to bring England's "second sons" to America. The Headright system allowed anyone who paid for an immigrant's transportation, to earn 50 acres of land per immigrant. Designed to incent immigration, the governing body thought paying headrights for the transport of people would result in massive importation of new immigrants. Indentured Servants made up about 75% of early immigrants and provided labor for the growing plantations. Increased population was important to further stabilize England's claim from Spain and/or France to an area of New America by having more permanent settlements.

In brief, the process for redeeming headrights involved having an individual earn headright(s) by providing a list of names of those for whom he had paid passage (confirmed by the passenger list of the transporting ship). The next step to gaining a patent for headrights was to select the available land he wanted to own. He then paid for a surveyor to survey the land requested, noting landmarks like rivers, creeks, and types of trees before the actual patent was awarded. Given the potential for error, there were many disputes over land boundaries which is part of the reason the Parish Vestrymen ordered the "processioning" of land every four years to have people go out and physically verify the neighboring boundaries. These processioning records for the surname "Dumas" mention his land as a landmark for districts within the same precinct as the DePriests which proved very useful to identifying the DePriest location.

Robert DePriest is documented as owning 350 acres in the St. Peter's Parish processioning of 1704, though an actual record of either his land description or the names of the people he sponsored as immigrants has not been found. It is very likely that he acquired the land from the original grantee via "transfer" (sale) of land already claimed under an original (government issued) patent. Such "transfers" (sales) of plats of land were documented only at a local (county/parish) level with no back up sent to England. There is very little evidence that these "purchases" are still extant. If the quit rents (taxes) were paid, the King didn't care how the original grantee divided his land or how much the grantee made as a land speculator.

Headrights could be bought and sold. Small plots of land could be "sold" *(transferred)* by large, patented land speculators to a yeoman *(farmer with small acreage amount)*. Alternatively, a land speculator could "buy" small quantities of headright certificates worth 50 acres each and then accumulate these small number of headright certificates to be granted more bulk plats of land to make even more profit from land speculation. There are many surviving documents showing the same person being granted different acreages in multiples of 50.

Even without extant proof of a land patent to Robert DePriest, one can still make a fairly accurate identification of where the DePriest land was located by comparing the land descriptions of the neighbors' patents and using old maps along with current day maps with surviving landmarks. Traditionally, changes in possession of PATENTED land were documented in the parish vestry. The same plot of land often passed through several surname ownerships created by abandonment of a patent which was often caused by death of the grantee *(called escheated land)*.

Observation: Much time has been spent by genealogists looking for yeoman land patents that don't exist!

Why Find Specific Land Location?

One reason for genealogists to get to know where their ancestor's land was located is that most people married those within their parish boundaries – not for religious reasons (everyone in 17th Century Virginia was <u>REQUIRED</u> to belong to the Church of England) but for proximal practicality. Most people married someone who lived within three miles of each other, which makes sense since that represented about a 3-hour walk (based on the average distance on foot or horse was 15-20 miles/day). It was also common for siblings of one family to marry siblings of another close family.

Note: Identifying a wife's first name is easy, but finding the maiden name of a female ancestor is often extremely difficult. It may sometimes be derived by finding the birthdates of matching candidates within a particular parish with a known given name to isolate some possibilities of a woman with a similar birth date to an eligible man.
Note: Many dates of birth were documented in parish registers, but not all of them.

For example, though there is no marriage record in the Parish Register of Robert's DePriest's son, Guillaume DePriest, he is known to have married a "Judith" via surviving documents regarding Guillaume's estate.

The typical marriage age range for couples in colonial times was about five years apart, with the groom typically being the elder. The typical marriage age for a colonial man was about 25. Still, it was closer to 30 in Virginia to allow time to work off his indenture and prove he could financially provide for a wife and family.

Note: If either the bride or groom lived outside of the parish, it was so specified as an exception, e.g., John Smith "of Henrico County" (to indicate John Smith lived outside the bounds of the (St. Peter's) parish)

Daughters' surnames were often used in the parish records for their births, but they were lost after that occasion.

So, searching the St. Peter's parish list of daughters named "Judith" born within about 5-10 years of Guillaume's birth of 1689 yields a list of likely candidates who could have possibly been the Judith known to have married Guillaume DePriest.

Only one Judith met the criteria; however, there could have been another Judith born into the parish who was not documented in the St. Peter's parish registry—or the birth or birth dates of Judiths in the St. Peter's parish are undecipherable. (There were also omissions of known children of parish members found in other documents.)

Although I lean toward "Renalls" as Judith's maiden name, as there is a Judith born to Thomas Renalls in 1688, there was another Judith born to another Huguenot with a birth year showing "168_." However, this record was Judith Strange, and she is found to have married a Poindexter. Another possibility is a Judith born to Amer Via; however, little is documented about Amer except that he is recognized as a registered Huguenot.

Why Identify Misspellings of Ancestor's Surname?

In the 17th century it often occurred that people with similar, but not the exact same surnames appear in various documents. Consider that in such a relatively small community of approximately 450 landowners in New Kent County as of 1704; it was doubtful to find <u>both</u> a Robert Depress and a Robert DePriest, a Robert Hues and a Robert Hughes, an Alexander Strainge and an Alexander Strange, a William Clayborn and a William Claiborne, a David Crafford and a David Crawford. etc., Tracing similar surnames can be historically revealing when similar but different spellings refer to the same person.

Example: Apperson and Epperson are two <u>different</u> surnames *(not just misspellings)*. That conclusion was made based on each having a record of a child born in the same year as shown:

Apperson (recognized Huguenot)	Epperson
	Pall son of **Jn"** Eperson 33 baptized the 25 Feb., 1 699-1700.
Frances Daughter of **Tho**. Apperson Born Baptized April 1st, *year?*	John son of W™ Eppeson 33 baptized the 19 Sept. 1703.
Frances Daughter of **Jn°** Apperson born December ye 3rd, 1706.	William son of Thomas 8z Elizabeth Epperson Bapt. Ye 20th of
Elizabeth Daughter of Jn° Apperson Born April ye 27th, 1708.	Elizabeth Daughter of Jn° Epperson bap' June ye 13th, 1708.
Anne Daughter of Jn" Apperson Born March ye 19th, 1710-11.	
Henry son of W" Apperson Born March ye 29th, 1713.	
John son of J"" Apperson Ju' Born Feb. ye 4th 2nd Mar. 2i.st, 1713.	
Elizabeth Daughter of W™ Apperson Born ye 17th of 7'", 17 15.	
Mary Daughter of Jn" Apperson Born February 26th, 1715.	

Observation: John and William were by far the most common given names for males in 17th-century Virginia, while Elizabeth and Mary were by far the most common female names.

Why Identify Neighbors of an Ancestor?

Given that travel in early Virginia was very restricted (an average distance traveled was only 15-20 miles per day) and that relatives, friends, and neighbors tended to travel together), it is helpful to learn more about the pertinent people, places, and events of the time. I used this data to make better assumptions/speculations about settlers' motivation in New Kent, including my Progenitor, Robert DePriest.

Death and re-marriage were very common, and physical proximity had to be a consideration when marrying or remarrying. The death rate in Virginia from disease alone was staggering in the first two decades, and death in childbirth was widespread. Identifying parish neighbors helps try to determine maiden names and track re-marriages of colonial women and men.

Why Are Colonial Maiden Names So Illusive?

In the 17th (and 18th to mid 19th Century), a woman's maiden name often got lost once she married. According to the law at the time, after marriage, a woman basically became a possession of her husband, and anything she owned became his property. So, if married, women were cited only as "first name, **wife of** (husband's full name)

: **e.g. Eliz: wife of Robert DePriest**"

Some given names, such as "Mary" and "Elizabeth," were so common that having only those first names to work with is typically worthless in tracking female ancestors of the 17th century.

34

One source that can help verify maiden names is a father's will. In colonial wills, daughters were typically referred to by their married name. This allows one to infer that her maiden name matched the father's in a will, leaving her some inheritance (often money or personal assets, but seldom land).

Why Identify Events Occurring Around Similar Dates?

It is helpful to group immigrants by common immigration dates, survival dates, land purchase dates, marriage dates, or children's birth dates to determine the likelihood that they were friends or family of the ancestor under study.

For example, a Huguenot with the surname "Dumas" appeared on the New Kent processioning of 1704 but hadn't been there in 1689. Surviving documents show Jerome Dumas came over in 1700 with the large Huguenot Refugee transport from London but did not settle in Manakintown as was the intended settlement spot for these Huguenots. Rather than accepting the governor's free land offered in Manakintown, Dumas settled on private land of 250 acres directly adjacent to Huguenot Robert DePriest per the 1704 quit rents listing for St. Peter's Parish. Huguenot-to-Huguenot closeness implies friendship that likely developed from being physically close during a previous time in life. Dumas is documented as arriving in Virginia from London in 1700, which hints *(but does not prove)* that Robert DePriest also emigrated to Virginia from London, creating a logical direction for more inquiries.

Land records of the pertinent people identified in the 1689 processioning list were used to gather an overview of who lived next to whom. By comparing surnames in the 1689 list with the 1704 and subsequent quit rents (tax lists), it can be determined when Robert DePriest died, even though there is no death record per se. His death range is based on his appearance on the processioning list in 1708 and the appearance of a "Widow

DePriest" in a subsequent 1711/12 processioning list for the same precinct. (i.e., **proof** that he died between 1708 and 1711 even though his death record is not mentioned in the Parish register).

Was There a French Connection in New Kent County Before 1700?

Because of the history of religious persecution of Huguenots, most French immigrants tried to assimilate into the English culture of America as quickly as possible. Though other ethnicities tended to immigrate into culturally similar neighborhoods, the French had experienced the slaughter of their fellow countrymen for simply wanting to be Protestant during the 16th and 17th Centuries in Catholic France. These Huguenots likely did not wish to be identified as "different" from their English neighbors. Early (*before 1700)*, Frenchmen most likely already spoke fluent English before immigrating as they had lived in England or the Channel Islands before migrating to Virginia.

Observation: Huguenot Cornelius Dabney and several other Huguenots served as Indian Interpreters. Since they were already bilingual, it would make sense that they could learn an Indian language more easily than someone who was not bilingual. Dabney lived north of the Pamunkey River next to the land reserved for the Pamunkey Indian Tribe and has documented dealings with them.

Between 1700 and 1702, a large transport of Huguenots sponsored by London sailed to Virginia on three different ships to carry about 700 London Huguenot refugees to a place south of the James River called Manakintown. England paid for these transports, and the King donated 10,000 acres of land to help these French refugees thrive in America. This seemingly kind gesture was primarily to relieve London of congestion caused by the influx of a large volume of French refugees caused by the 1687 Revocation of the Edict of Nantes and to provide a buffer zone between the current English Settlers and the local Indians.

Huguenot DePriest has surviving parish records to **prove** that he had been in Virginia 13 years <u>before</u> the frequently referenced "Manakintown Huguenots."

Found in the St. Peter's Parish Register:

> *"Guillaume (William) sone to Rob' Depress bap. Ye 24th of October, 168-.*
> *Eliz: wife of Rob' Depress Departed this life Sept. 27, 1689."*
> *Note: (Mother, Elizabeth, died shortly after childbirth with the date clearly stated above)*

Given that early settlers tended to move with relatives, friends, and other neighbors during the 17th and 18th Centuries, I sought to find out more about other Frenchmen in Virginia who likely played a part in the lives of the DePriests. An interesting discovery was made via early Parish records, showing that there were two key French Huguenots who were leaders in New Kent from its early beginnings.

The culture of New Kent County

Virginia was heavily influenced by Governor William Berkely and his Elite Cavaliers, but another culture grew out of the desire for more land. The land west of Jamestown was considered wilderness, and the special adventurous sorts were willing to risk the unknowns. There was the threat of Indian aggression, but what else? The thirst for new, unimproved land was stronger than their fears.

New Kent landowners were central to Bacon's Rebellion of 1676. Bacon opposed Governor Berkeley's negotiations with the Indians to limit the encroachment into Indian lands. The Rebellion occurred because young Francis Bacon didn't think the government was supportive enough to foster westward expansion. It took courage to

Now, review the response from Chatbot-3.5 to the same questions.

An important feature of AI is that it is forever learning and getting better. What it may not "know" today may well be a capability tomorrow. All of the responses reported below are untouched from Aimy's response.

Why Would Any English Gentlemen Go to Virginia in the 17th Century?

ChatGPT-3.5 A OD 06/24/2024

In the 17th century, English gentlemen, often members of the gentry or aristocracy, ventured to Virginia for various reasons. These motivations can be broadly categorized into economic opportunities, social ambitions, political circumstances, and personal reasons. Here's an in-depth look at why English gentlemen might choose to go to Virginia during this period:

Economic Opportunities

1. ***Land Grants and Wealth***: *Virginia offered the promise of substantial land grants. The headright system allowed individuals to acquire large tracts of land based on*

the number of people they transported to the colony. Land ownership was a path to wealth and status.

2. **Tobacco Cultivation**: *The cultivation of tobacco became a lucrative enterprise in Virginia. English gentlemen saw the potential for significant profits from tobacco farming, which required large estates and a labor force, often provided by indentured servants or enslaved Africans.*

3. **Investment and Speculation**: *Many gentlemen were investors in the Virginia Company of London, which sponsored early colonization efforts. By moving to Virginia, they could oversee their investments directly and participate in the management and development of the colony.*

Social Ambitions

1. **Establishing Estates**: *In England, opportunities for acquiring large estates were limited due to the entrenched nature of land ownership. In Virginia, gentlemen could establish new estates, build manor houses, and recreate the social hierarchy they were accustomed to in England.*

2. **Social Mobility**: *The New World offered opportunities for social mobility that were often not available in the more rigid class structures of England. Ambitious gentlemen could rise in social status through successful land management and business ventures.*

Political Circumstances

1. **Royalist Exiles**: *During the English Civil War (1642–1651) and the subsequent Commonwealth period, many Royalists (supporters of King Charles I) were displaced. Virginia, which remained loyal to the Crown for much of this period, became a haven for Royalist exiles seeking refuge and new beginnings.*

2. **Political Appointments**: *Some gentlemen were appointed to colonial administrative positions, such as governors, councilors, or other officials, by the Crown or*

colonial companies. These positions offered opportunities for power and influence in the burgeoning colony.

Personal Reasons

1. **Adventure and Exploration**: *The spirit of adventure and the allure of the unknown drew many to the New World. The prospect of exploring new territories and being part of the creation of a new society was enticing for many young gentlemen.*
2. **Religious Freedom**: *While less common among the Anglican gentry, some individuals sought greater religious freedom in the colonies. Dissenters and those wishing to practice their faith without persecution sometimes found the New World a more accommodating environment.*
3. **Escaping Debts or Scandal**: *Emigration to the colonies was sometimes a means of escaping debts, legal issues, or personal scandals. Starting anew in Virginia provided an opportunity to rebuild one's life away from the constraints and judgments of English society.*

Conclusion

The motivations for English gentlemen to venture to Virginia in the 17th century were diverse and multifaceted. The promise of economic gain, opportunities for social advancement, political exile, and personal ambitions or challenges all played roles in their decision to leave England for the New World. These motivations were instrumental in shaping the early development of Virginia and its society.

Why Is It Difficult to Track Ancestral Migration in 17th Century Virginia?

PROMPT: in genealogy research, Why Is It Difficult to Track Ancestral Migration in 17th Century Virginia

ChatGPT-3.5 as of 06/24/2024

Tracking ancestral migration in 17th-century Virginia is challenging due to several factors that complicate the genealogical research process. Here are the primary reasons why it is difficult to trace the movement of ancestors during this period:

1. Scarcity of Records

- ***Incomplete Records****: Many early records have been lost or were never created. Fires, wars, and natural disasters destroyed numerous colonial documents.*
- ***Limited Record Keeping****: In the 17th century, record-keeping practices were not as systematic or comprehensive as they are today. Records that do exist are often sparse and inconsistent.*

2. Fragmented Sources

- ***Varied Record Locations****: Records might be scattered across different jurisdictions, including county courthouses, churches, and private collections. This fragmentation makes it difficult to find all pertinent documents.*
- ***Inconsistent Record Formats****: The format and details recorded varied significantly, making it harder to extract consistent and reliable information.*

3. Common Names and Spellings

- ***Name Variations****: Spelling variations of names were common, as standardized spelling was not yet established. This can lead to difficulties in matching records to individuals.*
- ***Common Surnames****: Common surnames increase the difficulty distinguishing between individuals with the same or similar names.*

4. Geographical Mobility

- ***Frequent Moves****: Early settlers often moved frequently within the colony to find better land or opportunities, and these moves were not always well-documented.*

- *Migration Patterns*: Migration patterns were influenced by various factors, including economic opportunities, land grants, and conflicts with Native American tribes, but these movements were not always recorded.

5. Lack of Centralized Records

- *Decentralized Governance*: The colony was governed locally, with no centralized repository for records. This decentralization means researchers must search in multiple locations.
- *Parish Records*: While some church records exist, they are not comprehensive and may not cover all residents or events.

6. *Population Movement*

- *Indentured Servants and Slavery*: Many early settlers were indentured servants or enslaved individuals, whose movements were controlled by others and poorly documented.
- *Internal Migration*: As the population grew, families moved westward or to other colonies, further complicating the tracing of their movements.

7. Land Transactions

Land Grants and Patents: Land was often acquired through headrights, and these transactions were sometimes recorded, but the records might not survive or be complete.

Land Records: Existing land records can provide clues but often require extensive interpretation and cross-referencing with other documents.

8. Legal and Administrative Changes

- ***Changing Boundaries***: County and parish boundaries changed frequently as the colony expanded, and records may have been kept under different jurisdictions over time.

- ***Administrative Practices***: Administrative practices evolved, leading to variations in how and where records were kept.

Conclusion

Combining these factors creates significant challenges for genealogists trying to trace ancestral migrations in 17th-century Virginia. Successful research often requires piecing together fragments of information from a variety of sources, extensive cross-referencing, and sometimes a bit of luck. Despite the difficulties, persistence and thorough investigation can yield valuable insights into ancestral movements and life in early Virginia.

Why Focus on Surnames and Social Class of Landowners?

PROMPT: in genealogy research, Why Focus on Surnames and Social Class of Landowners

ChatCPT-3.5 as of 06/24/2024

Focusing on surnames and social class of landowners in genealogy research is crucial for several reasons. These aspects provide valuable context and insights that can help trace lineage, understand family history, and uncover connections that might not be immediately apparent. Here are the primary reasons for this focus:

1. Land Ownership as a Record Source

- ***Extensive Documentation***: Land transactions, grants, and deeds were meticulously recorded. These documents often contain names, dates, and other important details that can help establish family connections.
- ***Legal and Public Records***: As landownership was tied to legal and economic status, it generated numerous records in court and public offices. These records are often more complete and better preserved than other types of documents.

2. Social Status Indicators

- ***Economic Status***: Landowners were often of higher economic status, making their records more likely to be preserved and documented. Understanding their social class helps place ancestors in the broader historical and social context.
- ***Community Standing***: Social class influenced community roles and responsibilities, including political and civic duties. These roles generated additional records, such as wills, tax lists, and probate records.

3. Surname Clarity

Surname Consistency: Landowners' surnames were often recorded more consistently than those of non-landowners, reducing confusion due to spelling variations or alias use.

- ***Family Lineage***: Surnames help trace family lines over generations. Land records often indicate relationships between individuals (e.g., through inheritance), which can confirm family ties.

4. Land as a Source of Wealth and Power

- ***Economic Influence***: Land was a primary source of wealth and power. Understanding landownership patterns helps elucidate economic status and influence within the community.

- *Inheritance Patterns*: Land was commonly passed down through families, providing a trail of inheritance that can clarify familial connections and lineage.

5. Geographical Stability

- *Settlement Patterns*: Landowners were more likely to have established roots in a particular area, making it easier to trace their movements and family history within that region.
- *Local Records*: Records of land transactions and ownership are often kept locally, making it easier to locate relevant documents within specific areas.

6. Connecting Families and Communities

- *Neighboring Landowners*: Researching the surnames and social class of neighboring landowners can reveal connections between families, such as intermarriages and social alliances.
- *Community Networks*: Landownership can illuminate social networks within a community, helping to understand how families interacted and supported one another.

7. Historical Context

- *Colonial and Early American History*: Landownership patterns reflect broader historical trends, such as colonization, settlement expansion, and economic development. This context enriches understanding of ancestors' lives.
- *Migration Patterns*: Land records can indicate migration patterns, showing how and why families moved within or between regions.

8. Documenting Large Estates

- ***Plantation Records***: *In regions where plantations were common, records often detailed extensive information about landowners, their families, and even enslaved individuals, providing a wealth of genealogical data.*

- ***Estate Inventories***: *Detailed inventories of large estates can offer insights into the daily lives and economic activities of landowners and their families.*

Conclusion

Focusing on the surnames and social class of landowners in genealogy research is a strategic approach that leverages the abundance of available records and the stability associated with land ownership. This focus provides a solid foundation for building family trees, understanding historical context, and uncovering the intricate web of relationships that define family histories. By tracing land ownership and associated social status, genealogists can piece together a more accurate and comprehensive picture of their ancestors' lives and legacies.

Why Identify the Amount of Acreage Owned?

PROMPT: in genealogy research, Why Identify the Amount of Acreage Owned

ChatCPT-3.5 as of 06/24/2024

Identifying the amount of acreage owned by ancestors in genealogy research can provide valuable insights and context for understanding their lives and historical circumstances. Here are several reasons why this information is important:

1. ***Wealth and Social Status***: *The amount of land owned often correlates with wealth and social standing in historical societies. Larger land holdings generally indicate a higher economic status, which can help place ancestors within the social hierarchy of their time.*

2. ***Legal and Financial Records***: *Land ownership is typically well-documented through deeds, land grants, tax records, and estate inventories. These records*

provide concrete evidence of property ownership and can offer details such as acreage, boundaries, and neighboring landowners.

3. ***Inheritance and Family Dynamics:*** *Acreage information can reveal patterns of inheritance within families. Tracking changes in land ownership over generations can shed light on family dynamics, inheritance laws, and the passing of wealth from one generation to the next.*

4. ***Economic Activities:*** *The size and type of land owned can indicate the economic activities of ancestors. For example, large agricultural holdings suggest involvement in farming or plantation activities, while smaller plots might be indicative of tradesmen or urban dwellers.*

5. ***Community and Relationships:*** *Acreage information can help identify relationships and connections within communities. Neighboring landowners, shared boundaries, and land transactions often reveal social networks, alliances, and intermarriages among families.*

6. ***Geographical Context:*** *Understanding the amount of acreage owned provides geographical context. It can help researchers locate ancestral lands, trace migration patterns, and identify areas where ancestors lived and worked.*

7. ***Historical Trends and Context:*** *Changes in land ownership patterns over time reflect broader historical trends such as colonization, westward expansion, land speculation, and economic shifts. Analyzing acreage data within historical contexts enriches the understanding of ancestors' lives.*

8. ***Land Use and Development:*** *Acreage information can offer insights into how land was used and developed. For example, changes in land size or usage may coincide with periods of agricultural expansion, urbanization, or industrialization.*

9. ***Legal and Property Rights****: Land ownership records often include details about property rights, land grants, boundaries, and legal disputes. These details can illuminate the legal status and rights of ancestors within their communities.*

In summary, identifying the amount of acreage owned by ancestors adds depth and specificity to genealogical research by providing information on wealth, social status, family dynamics, economic activities, community relationships, geographical context, historical trends, land use, and legal aspects. Combining this data with other genealogical records creates a more comprehensive understanding of ancestors' lives and legacies.

Why Find Specific Land Locations?

PROMPT: in genealogy research, Why Find Specific Land Locations

ChatCPT-3.5 as of 06/24/2024

Finding specific land locations is crucial in genealogy research for several reasons:

1. ***Geographical Context:*** *Knowing the exact location of ancestral land provides a geographical context for understanding where ancestors lived, worked, and interacted within their communities.*

2. ***Property Ownership:*** *Specific land locations confirm ownership and property boundaries, which are essential for tracing land ownership through generations and understanding inheritance patterns.*

3. ***Migration and Settlement:*** *Land locations help trace migration patterns and settlement movements of ancestors. It can reveal patterns of movement within regions or across different areas.*

4. ***Community Relationships:*** *Identifying neighboring properties and landmarks helps establish relationships with other families and communities. Shared boundaries and proximity to certain landmarks can indicate social networks and interactions.*

5. ***Historical Context:*** *Land locations within historical maps and documents offer insights into historical events, changes in land use, and developments in the local area. This context enriches the understanding of ancestors' lives.*

6. **Legal and Administrative Records:** *Specific land locations are recorded in legal documents such as deeds, land grants, surveys, and tax records. These records provide official documentation of property ownership and transactions.*

7. **Environmental Factors:** *Land locations may reveal information about the environmental factors that influenced ancestors' lives, such as proximity to water sources, agricultural land, natural resources, or industrial areas.*

8. **Urban vs. Rural Life:** *Knowing whether ancestors lived in urban centers or rural areas can provide insights into their occupations, lifestyles, and community involvement.*

9. **Cultural and Ethnic Communities**: *Land locations may be associated with specific cultural or ethnic communities, indicating heritage, traditions, and social connections.*

10. **Genealogical Evidence:** *Specific land locations serve as valuable evidence in genealogical research, corroborating other sources of information and helping to construct a comprehensive family history.*

In summary, finding specific land locations enhances genealogical research by providing geographical context, confirming property ownership, tracing migration patterns, establishing community relationships, understanding historical context, accessing legal records, considering environmental factors, exploring urban-rural distinctions, recognizing cultural communities, and strengthening genealogical evidence.

Why Identify Misspellings of Ancestors' Surnames?

PROMPT: in genealogy research, Why Identify Misspellings of Ancestors' Surnames

ChatCPT-3.5 as of 06/24/2024

In genealogy research, identifying misspellings of ancestors' surnames is crucial for several reasons:

1. ***Historical Inconsistencies:*** *During earlier centuries, literacy rates were lower, and standardized spelling was not common. As a result, names were often recorded phonetically based on how they were heard by the recorder, leading to various spellings of the same name.*

2. ***Record Keeping Practices:*** *Different clerks and recorders might spell names differently. Understanding the possible variations in spellings can help genealogists locate records that might otherwise be missed if only one spelling is considered.*

3. ***Migration and Assimilation:*** *Immigrants often faced language barriers, and their names were frequently anglicized or altered to fit the phonetic and spelling norms of their new country. Identifying these variations is essential for tracing immigrant ancestors.*

4. ***Regional Dialects and Accents:*** *Variations in regional dialects and accents can lead to different spellings of the same name. For example, a name might be spelled differently in various regions due to the local pronunciation.*

Why Identify Neighbors of an Ancestor?

PROMPT: in genealogy research, Why Identify Neighbors of an Ancestor
ChatCPT-3.5 as of 06/24/2-24

Identifying neighbors of an ancestor is an important aspect of genealogy research for several reasons:

1. ***Community and Social Networks:*** *Neighbors often played significant roles in each other's lives, especially in close-knit communities. Understanding these relationships can provide insights into the social dynamics and support networks of your ancestors.*

2. ***Migration Patterns:*** *Families and neighbors often migrated together. Identifying neighbors can help trace migration patterns and discover where your ancestors might have moved from or to.*

3. *Marriage Connections*: Neighbors frequently intermarried. By identifying neighbors, you might discover connections to other families that became relatives through marriage.

4. *Shared Documentation:* Neighbors may appear together in various records such as censuses, land deeds, church registers, and wills. Knowing who the neighbors were can help verify the identity of your ancestor in these records.

5. *Collateral Research:* Sometimes, records for your direct ancestor may be missing or incomplete. Researching the neighbors can provide indirect evidence and help piece together information about your ancestor.

6. *Land Transactions:* Neighbors often bought, sold, or inherited land from each other. Land records can reveal much about relationships, economic status, and the movement of families over time.

7. *Census Accuracy:* Enumerators might record neighbors in sequence on census records. Identifying neighbors can help confirm the correct location and household if names are misspelled or hard to read.

8. *Community History*: Understanding the broader community in which your ancestor lived can provide context to their life. It can reveal what life was like, the challenges they faced, and the opportunities available to them.

9. *Witnesses and Sponsors:* Neighbors often served as witnesses in legal documents or as sponsors at events like baptisms and weddings. Their presence can lend credibility to your ancestor's records and help build a more complete family story.

10. *Problem Solving*: If you hit a brick wall in your research, looking at the neighbors might provide new clues. Neighbors could share surnames, origins, or other characteristics that lead to breakthroughs.

11. *Cultural and Ethnic Clues:* Neighbors might share cultural, ethnic, or linguistic backgrounds with your ancestor. This can help identify your ancestor's origins and community affiliations.

12. *Economic and Occupational Insights*: Neighbors might work together or be involved in similar trades. Understanding these connections can shed light on your ancestor's occupation and economic status.

In summary, identifying neighbors of an ancestor enriches genealogical research by uncovering social connections, migration patterns, and additional sources of information that might not be immediately apparent when focusing solely on direct ancestors.

Why Are Colonial Maiden Names So Elusive?

PROMPT: in genealogy research, Why Are Colonial Maiden Names So Elusive?
ChatGPT-3.5 as of 06/24/2024

Colonial maiden names are often elusive in genealogy research due to several factors:

1. **Patriarchal Naming Conventions:** *During the colonial period, society was predominantly patriarchal. Women were often identified in relation to their fathers or husbands, and their maiden names were rarely recorded. Official documents frequently referred to women by their married names.*

2. **Lack of Record Keeping:** *Many records from the colonial period either did not survive or were not kept in the first place. Events like fires, wars, and natural deterioration have led to the loss of many early records that might have contained maiden names.*

3. **Sparse Documentation of Women:** *Women were less frequently mentioned in legal and official documents compared to men. When women were mentioned, it was often in relation to their husbands or fathers, and their maiden names were often omitted.*

4. **Church Records and Customs:** *Church records, which are a primary source of genealogical information, often focused on the male head of the household. Baptismal, marriage, and burial records might not always include maiden names.*

5. ***Property and Legal Rights:*** *In many colonial societies, women had limited property and legal rights. As a result, they were less likely to appear in property deeds, wills, and other legal documents that might have included their maiden names.*

6. ***Changes in Surnames***: *Upon marriage, women typically adopted their husbands' surnames. If a woman married more than once due to widowhood or other reasons, tracking her maiden name through multiple surname changes can be challenging.*

7. ***Informal Naming Practices:*** *In some communities, especially smaller or rural ones, informal naming practices were common. Nicknames, variations in spelling, and the use of middle names instead of maiden names can complicate the identification process.*

8. ***Cultural Practices:*** *Different cultural practices influenced how names were recorded. For example, in some cultures, it was customary to use only first names or to not emphasize maiden names, making it harder to trace these names in the records.*

9. ***Limited Access to Sources:*** *Some sources that might contain maiden names, such as personal letters, diaries, and family Bibles, are not always available to researchers. These private records often remain within families and are not accessible through public archives.*

10. ***Commonality of Names***: *Common surnames and given names can create confusion. Distinguishing between multiple women with the same or similar names in the same area requires additional evidence, which is often not available.*

11. ***Language Barriers***: *In colonial America, records might be written in various languages depending on the colonial power (e.g., English, Spanish, Dutch, French). Language barriers and translations can lead to the loss or alteration of maiden names.*

12. ***Misinterpretation of Records:*** *Early records were often handwritten and can be difficult to read due to the handwriting style of the time. Misinterpretation of these records can result in incorrect assumptions about maiden names.*

Strategies to Overcome Challenges

1. ***Examine Multiple Sources****: Look for maiden names in a variety of sources, including wills, probate records, land deeds, church records, and tax lists.*
2. ***Family and Community Context****: Research the broader family and community to identify patterns and connections that might reveal a maiden name.*
3. ***Collaborate with Other Researchers****: Connect with other genealogists researching the same families or areas. They might have access to different records or insights.*
4. ***Genetic Genealogy****: DNA testing can provide clues to maiden names by identifying genetic matches that lead to previously unknown branches of a family.*

By understanding these challenges and employing a variety of research strategies, genealogists can improve their chances of uncovering elusive colonial maiden names.

Why Identify Events Around Similar Dates?

Identifying events around similar dates in genealogy research is crucial for several reasons:

1. ***Contextual Understanding:*** *Understanding the context in which your ancestors lived can provide valuable insights into their lives. Events such as wars, migrations, epidemics, economic changes, and natural disasters could have significantly influenced their decisions and circumstances.*

2. ***Verification of Records:*** *Comparing events around similar dates can help verify the accuracy of records. If multiple records show significant life events (births, marriages, deaths) happening at the same time, it can confirm the identity of the individuals involved.*

3. ***Family Connections:*** *Events around similar dates can reveal family connections. For example, marriages and the birth of children often follow each other closely. Identifying these events can help construct a more accurate family tree and understand family dynamics.*

4. ***Migration Patterns:*** *Understanding migration patterns can be crucial in genealogy. Identifying events around similar dates can reveal why and when an ancestor moved from one place to another. This could be due to economic opportunities, political unrest, or other significant events.*

5. ***Social and Cultural Practices:*** *Identifying events around similar dates can provide insights into social and cultural practices. For instance, marriage customs, religious ceremonies, and community events can be better understood when placed in their temporal context.*

6. ***Legal and Property Transactions:*** *Many legal and property transactions are tied to specific events. Wills, deeds, and other legal documents often reference significant life events like marriages, births, and deaths. Identifying these dates can help locate and understand these documents.*

7. ***Cross-referencing Records:*** *Identifying events around similar dates allows for cross-referencing multiple sources. This can help corroborate information from different records, such as census data, church records, and civil registrations, ensuring a more accurate genealogical profile.*

8. ***Tracking Changes Over Time:*** *Understanding events around similar dates helps track changes in an ancestor's life over time. This can include changes in occupation, social status, and geographic location, providing a more comprehensive view of their life.*

9. ***Identifying Patterns and Trends***: Identifying events around similar dates can reveal patterns and trends within a family or community. For instance, patterns of naming, marriage ages, or occupational changes can provide deeper insights into family history.

10. ***Locating Ancestors in Time and Place:*** Precise identification of events around similar dates can help pinpoint where and when an ancestor lived, aiding in the search for additional records and evidence.

Strategies to Identify Events Around Similar Dates

1. ***Create a Timeline***: Construct a timeline of significant events in an ancestor's life, including births, marriages, deaths, migrations, and other relevant events. This helps visualize their life and identify patterns or gaps.

2. ***Consult Multiple Sources***: Use various record types such as census records, church registers, civil registrations, newspapers, and land records to find events. Cross-reference these sources to ensure accuracy.

3. ***Look for Related Records***: When you find a significant event, look for related records. For example, a marriage record might lead to the discovery of baptismal records for children or property records related to the family.

4. ***Use Historical Context***: Research the historical context of the time. Understanding broader historical events can provide clues about why certain events happened when they did.

5. ***Community and Family Studies***: Study the broader community and extended family. Events in the lives of neighbors or relatives can provide context and additional information about your direct ancestors.

By identifying and understanding events around similar dates, genealogists can construct a richer, more accurate family history, providing deeper insights into the lives and times of their ancestors.

ChatCPT-3.5 as of 06/24/2024

In the context of genealogy research, identifying a French connection in New Kent County, Virginia, before 1700 can be quite intriguing and requires understanding the historical and socio-political context of the time. Here are some points to consider:

Historical Context

1. **Huguenot Migration:** *The most significant French connection in Virginia before 1700 involves the Huguenots, French Protestants who fled religious persecution in France. The Edict of Nantes, which had granted them some religious freedoms, was revoked in 1685, leading to increased persecution and migration.*

2. **Manakin Settlement:** *The most well-known Huguenot settlement in Virginia was the Manakin Town on the James River, established in the 1690s in what is now Powhatan County, near New Kent County. While this settlement postdates the 1700 mark, it indicates a French presence and migration patterns that could have impacted New Kent County as well.*

Researching French Connections in New Kent County

1. **Church Records***: French Huguenots often established their own churches or attended Anglican services when no French church was available. Searching through early church records in New Kent County might reveal French names or references to French families.*

2. **Land Grants and Patents***: The Virginia colonial government granted land to settlers, including Huguenots. Examining land grant records can help identify French settlers in New Kent County before 1700.*

3. ***Census and Tax Records****:* Although comprehensive census records from this period are scarce, tax records, tithable lists, and militia rolls might contain references to French settlers.

4. ***Colonial Records and Correspondence****:* Letters, official correspondence, and colonial records sometimes mention notable settlers and events. These documents can provide clues about the presence of French families in the area.

5. ***Family Histories and Local Histories:*** Published family histories and local histories often include references to early settlers. These secondary sources can provide leads and context for identifying French connections.

Examples and Notable Individuals

1. ***Huguenot Families****:* Some notable Huguenot families that settled in Virginia and could have connections to New Kent County include the Fontaine, Maury, and Dupuy families. Tracking the movements of these families can help identify connections to New Kent County.

2. ***French Influence on Names****:* Early settlers sometimes anglicized their names. Identifying original French surnames and their variations can help locate records of French settlers.

3. ***Migration Patterns****:* Understanding migration patterns from other colonies (like Maryland or South Carolina) where French Huguenots initially settled can provide context for their movements into Virginia.

Conclusion

While direct evidence of a French connection in New Kent County, Virginia, before 1700 might be sparse, the broader historical context and available records can help trace these connections. Huguenot migrations, land grants, church records, and local histories are valuable resources in uncovering any French ancestry in the region. By piecing together these records and understanding the historical backdrop, genealogists can uncover the presence and influence of French settlers in New Kent County during the colonial period.

Observations Comparing "The Book" Original Content And Aimy's Version:

"The Book" includes footnotes that identify specific sources of information, allowing for thorough verification. It also incorporates maps and graphics to enhance the understanding of the material presented. Currently, ChatGPT is limited to textual content, so any maps or graphics would need to be manually found or created and inserted.

Aimy's version is excellent for guiding genealogists on various aspects of the topic and suggesting directions for further research. While the "facts" provided by Aimy would need to be verified through inspection, Aimy offers an excellent starting point for investigation. Below are contrasting examples, categorized according to the structure of "The Book" (i.e., Places, Events, People, Methods). Each section first shows an extract from "The Book," followed by Aimy's write-up on the same topic.

Category PLACES - Geographic Overview of the Virginia Colony

From "The Book"

The Development of Virginia started around the banks of the James River and spread out from there to the nearby rivers, i.e., the York, Pamunkey, Chickahominy, and Mattaponi. This land was partitioned into four incorporated areas, then into 8 "shires," then, as the population grew, it was divided into 14 counties by 1704. The "quitrents" (tax lists) of 1704 only considered these 14 counties under Royal control, and their "quitrents" were to be paid to the King for governance and protection against local Indian tribes.

Significant Rivers Around New Kent

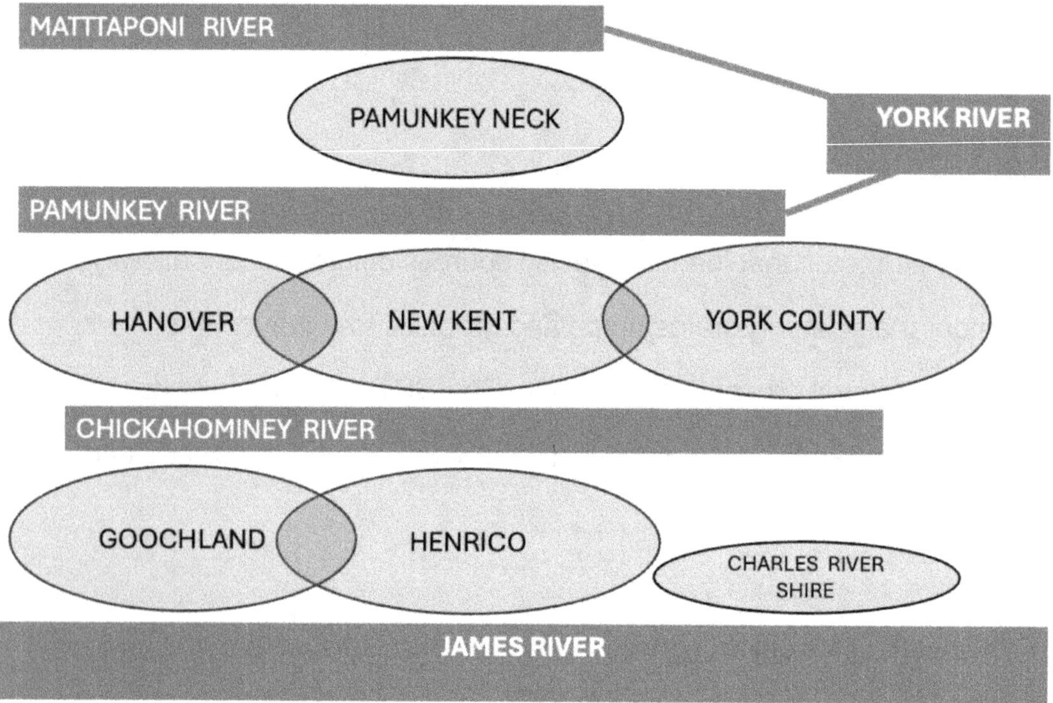

Travel modes in the 17th century were by foot, horse, or water. Rivers were the superhighways of the time. Early Settlers needed access to water to take their products to market. Tobacco, the money crop, was heavy and rolled over land in "hogs heads" to access water.

The York River split in two, and the southern branch was renamed the Pamunkey River, which became the northern border of New Kent County.

The map below shows the area highlighted in contrast to a broader view of the colony with major rivers named.

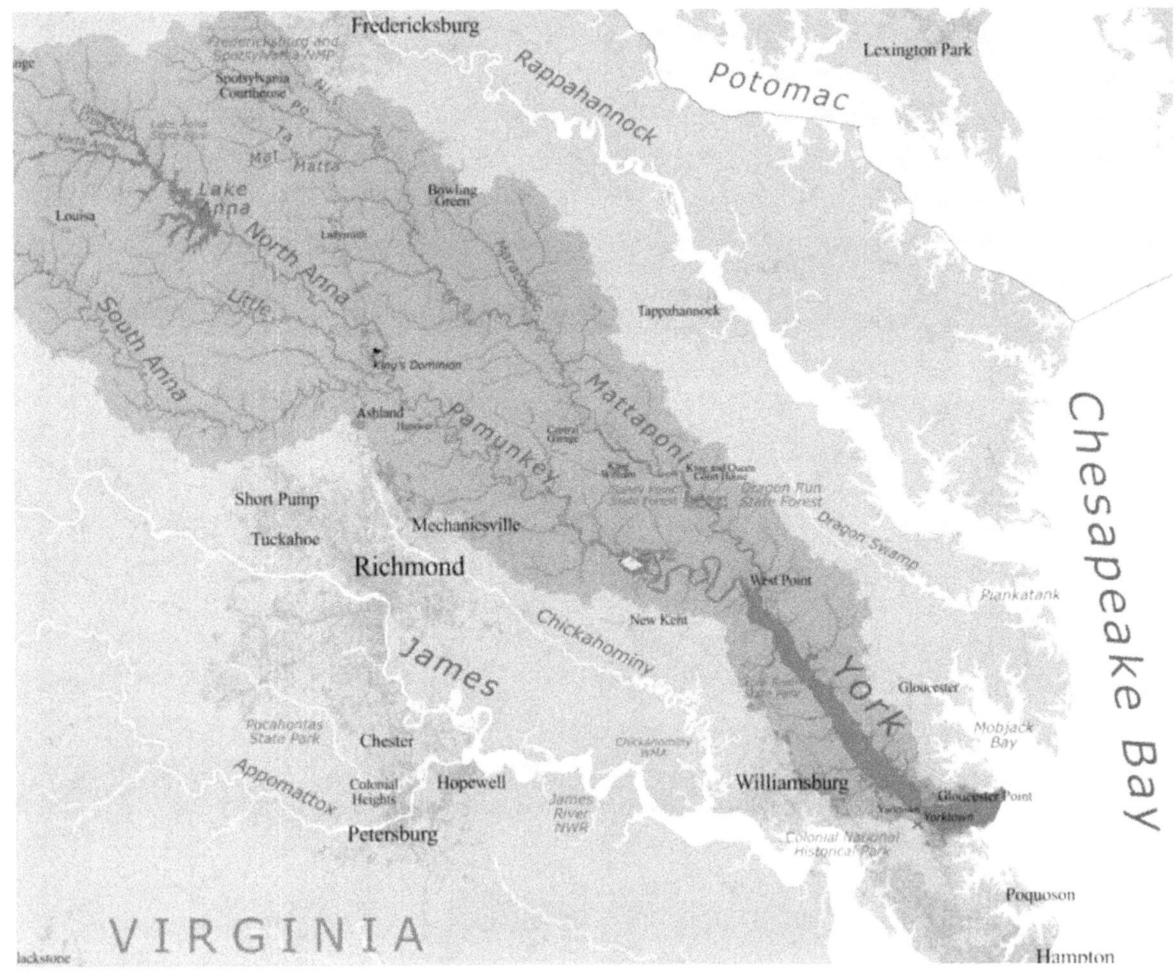

The area of Interest is roughly between the James and York Rivers.

The Northern Neck

Much further north, around the Rappahannock and Potomac Rivers, was unchartered territory referred to as "The Northern Neck," which is outside the scope of this study.

In September 1649, King Charles II of England granted land to seven Englishmen of Virginia between the Rappahannock and Potomac Rivers as a "Proprietary." See the Map below.

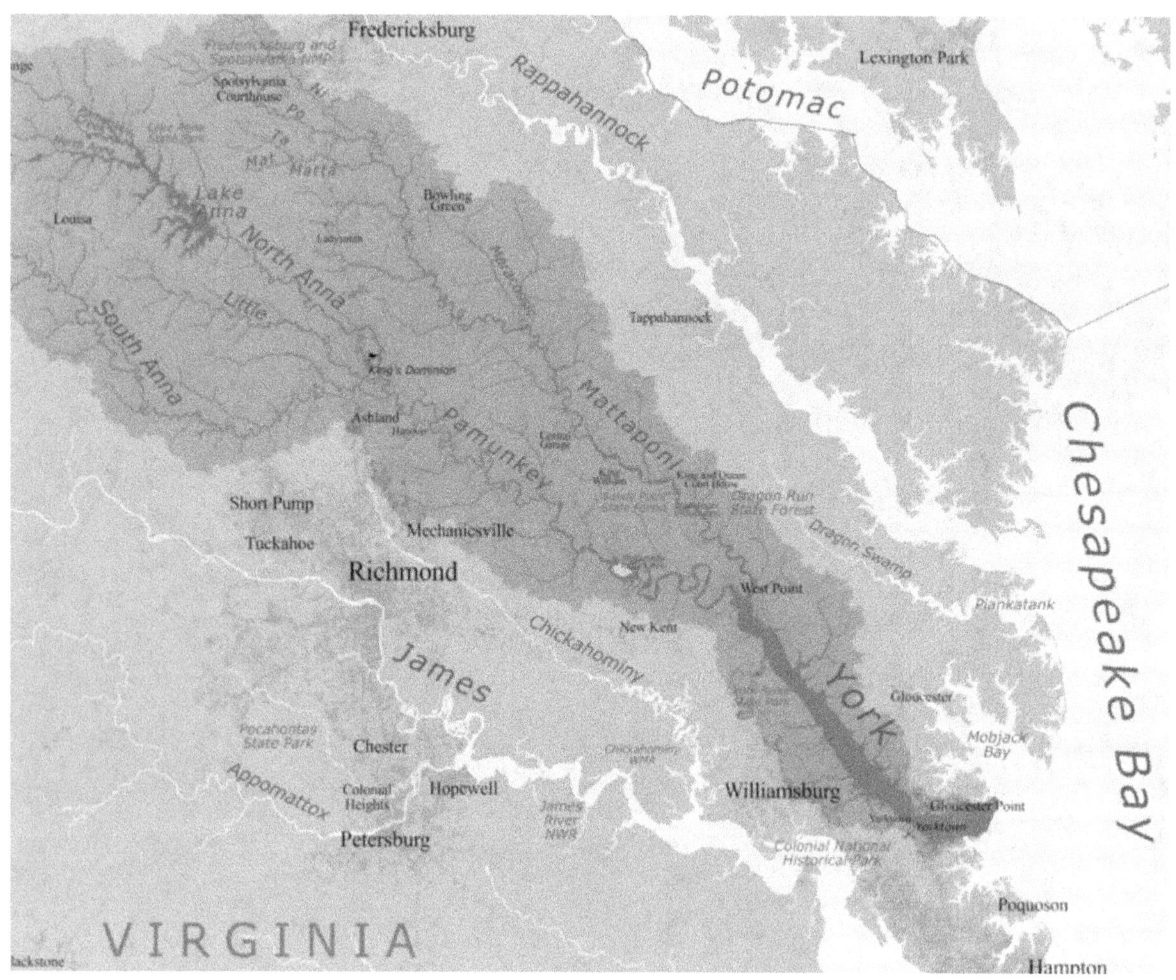

"Proprietary" meant that the seven selected Englishmen could run it as they pleased and expect no support from the Crown. As such, they were free to form their government systems and collect taxes for themselves, not for the king. Surnames most associated with this adventure are Culpepper and Fairfax.

The King or the grantees hardly recognized the extent of the Northern Neck grants because most had never been mapped. Due to political struggles in England, the proprietors thought little of their grant since Charles II was a king without a kingdom. The Northern Neck proprietary was short-lived and is out of the scope of this research, but it is mentioned to understand why only the 14 Royal Colonies/ Counties were examined in the 1704 "census."

Places - Aimy's version:

PROMPT: as a genealogist, provide a Geographic Overview of the Virginia Colony

ChatGPT-3.5 as of 06/27/2024

Geographic Overview of the Virginia Colony

Location and Early Settlements

The Virginia Colony, established in 1607, was the first permanent English settlement in North America. Located on the eastern seaboard, it encompassed a broad area that now includes the modern state of Virginia and parts of neighboring states.

Natural Features

- *Chesapeake Bay: This large estuary was crucial to the colony's development, providing a natural harbor, abundant seafood, and facilitating trade and transportation.*
- *James River: One of the most significant rivers in the colony, the James River provided a vital route for exploration, trade, and settlement. Jamestown, the first permanent settlement, was established on its banks.*
- *Potomac River: Forming part of the colony's northern boundary, the Potomac River was another important waterway for transport and trade.*
- *Appalachian Mountains: The western boundary of the colony was defined by the Appalachian Mountains, which were a barrier to early westward expansion but later became a source of natural resources.*

Climate

- *Mild Winters and Hot Summers: Virginia's climate was characterized by mild winters and hot, humid summers, which were conducive to the growth of tobacco, the colony's primary cash crop.*
- *Rich Soil: The fertile soil, particularly in the Tidewater region, was ideal for agriculture and contributed to the colony's prosperity.*

Regions of the Virginia Colony

1. *Tidewater Region:*

- *Description*: This coastal area along the Chesapeake Bay and the Atlantic Ocean included the earliest settlements.
  - *Importance*: Known for its fertile soil and extensive plantations, the Tidewater region was the heart of Virginia's tobacco economy.

2. *Piedmont Region*:
   - *Description*: Located west of the Tidewater, the Piedmont region features rolling hills and fertile valleys.
   - *Importance*: As settlers moved inland, the Piedmont became an important area for tobacco plantations and later diversified agriculture.

3. *Blue Ridge Mountains*:
   - *Description*: This mountain range forms part of the Appalachian Mountains and runs through western Virginia.
   - *Importance*: The Blue Ridge Mountains served as a natural barrier to westward expansion but also provided timber and mineral resources.

4. *Valley and Ridge Region*:
   - *Description*: West of the Blue Ridge Mountains, this region consists of long, parallel ridges and valleys.
   - *Importance*: Known for its rich farmland and strategic routes through the mountains, it became an important area for migration and settlement.

5. *Appalachian Plateau*:
   - *Description*: The westernmost part of Virginia, characterized by rugged terrain and high elevations.
   - *Importance*: Less settled during the colonial period due to its challenging geography, but it later became important for mining and other industries.

Colonial Settlements and Counties

- *Jamestown*: Founded in 1607 on the James River, it was the first permanent English settlement.

- *Williamsburg*: Established as the capital in 1699, it became a cultural and political center.
- *Richmond*: Founded in 1737, Richmond became an important trading and administrative center.

Expansion and Development

- *County Formation*: As the population grew, the colony was divided into counties for administrative purposes. Each county had its own court, militia, and local government.
- *Plantation Economy*: The economy was dominated by large plantations, primarily producing tobacco for export to Europe. This led to the importation of indentured servants and, later, African slaves to provide labor.
- *Trade and Commerce*: The colony's economy was heavily reliant on trade, both with Native American tribes and across the Atlantic. Ports along the Chesapeake Bay facilitated the export of tobacco and import of goods.

Significance

The geography of the Virginia Colony played a crucial role in its development. The fertile soil and favorable climate allowed for successful agriculture, while the extensive waterways facilitated trade and communication. The varied terrain influenced settlement patterns and economic activities, contributing to the colony's growth and prosperity.

Understanding the geographic context of the Virginia Colony is essential for genealogists researching early American ancestors. It provides insight into the environmental and economic factors that shaped their lives and influenced migration patterns, settlement decisions, and social structures.

Category EVENTS: Bacon's Rebellion

As printed in "The Book," my synopsis has more detail, and content sources are cited. However, Aimy got it right and presented the information in a much more organized manner:

Except from "The Book"

Bacon's Rebellion was a significant event pitting the interests of discontented settlers and the Crown.

Extract from Virginia Museum of History and Culture:[3]

The economic disparity between the gentry in eastern Virginia and the growing number of small planters, poor immigrants, and freed servants living on the frontier led to substantial discontent among the lower and middle classes.

Many settlers wanted the Indians to be driven out of their land or be killed. Former servants believed that acquiring available land required taking it from the Indians. Governor Berkeley, on the other hand, wanted accommodation of friendly tribes.

Unlike most of his followers, Bacon was socially and politically prominent. Bacon commanded a volunteer militia and demanded a commission from the governor to fight the Indians, which Berkeley denied. Bacon proceeded to raid, loot, and kill despite Berkeley's refusal to recognize his vigilante group.

On July 30, 1676, Bacon issued a "Declaration in the Name of the People". His declaration was directed against Berkeley and the governing elite he charged were corrupt and negligent.

Bacon laid siege to the Jamestown, forcing Berkeley to flee. Determining he could neither hold the capital nor risk losing it again, Bacon burned Jamestown on September 19. The fire destroyed many houses, the church, and the statehouse.

---

[3]BACON'S REBELLION IN VIRGINIA IN THE YEARS 1675 & 1676 , Virginia Museum of History and Culture. https://virginiahistory.org/learn/bacons-rebellion-virginia-years-1675-1676#:~:text=Bacon's%20Rebellion%20failed%20to%20overturn,advance%20substantial%20demographic%20change%2C%20however. Accessed 5/2/2024.

While his primary enemy was Berkeley and his cronies, Bacon found an equal if not greater foe in the Indians. The Indians had been subjugated, and Berkeley and the elites no longer saw them as a threat. However, frontiersmen felt different security than did older planters in eastern Virginia.

October 26, 1676

Nathaniel Bacon dies of illness. The rebellion dissolves, and 23 of his supporters are executed, including William Drummond (a leader in the uprising), Giles Bland (Customs inspector), Anthony Arnold (largest landowner of the group with land in New Kent), and Thomas Hall (New Kent County clerk). [4]

Berkeley was removed as governor and called back to England, where he died shortly after that.

Bacon's Rebellion failed to overturn the established order in the colony. In fact, after the rebellion, the planter elite consolidated power and intensified the social inequalities that would characterize 18th-century Virginia. It did advance substantial demographic change, however. The population of enslaved Africans multiplied while that of white immigrants slowed. Racial unity between poor and wealthy whites was defined as the slave population grew, and racial distinctions became interwoven into the laws and social fabric of the colony. [5]

Aimy's version of Bacon's Rebellion

PROMPT: Using only online repositories, tell me the story of Bacon's Rebellion of 1676

ChatGPT-3.5 as of 06/24/2024

---

[4] Bacon's Rebellion, https://www.vagenweb.org/shenandoah/wars/bacons_rebellion.html Accessed 02/15/2024.

[5] BACON'S REBELLION IN VIRGINIA IN THE YEARS 1675 & 1676, https://virginiahistory.org/learn/bacons-rebellion-virginia-years-1675-1676#:~:text=Bacon's%20Rebellion%20failed%20to%20overturn,advance%20substantial%20demographic%20change%2C%20however Accessed 5/2/2024.

Bacon's Rebellion of 1676 was a significant event in colonial Virginia that highlighted tensions between colonists, Native Americans, and the colonial government. Here's a summary of the story using information from online repositories:

1. ***Background and Causes:***
   - *The colony of Virginia faced economic challenges, including high taxes and a lack of representation in the government.*
   - *Native American raids on the frontier were also a concern for settlers, who felt that the colonial government was not adequately protecting them.*
   - *Nathaniel Bacon, a wealthy planter, emerged as a leader of discontented colonists and small farmers who wanted more aggressive action against Native American tribes.*

2. ***Bacon's Leadership:***
   - *Bacon organized a militia of volunteers to defend against Native American attacks and launched several successful campaigns against Native American settlements.*
   - *However, Bacon's actions were not authorized by the colonial government, leading to tensions between him and Governor William Berkeley.*

3. ***Rebellion Erupts:***
   - *In 1676, Bacon and his supporters marched on Jamestown, the colonial capital, demanding reforms and a commission to continue their military actions against Native Americans.*
   - *Governor Berkeley initially agreed to some of their demands but later declared Bacon and his followers rebels and traitors.*

4. ***Conflict and Resolution:***
   - *Bacon's forces briefly controlled Jamestown but were eventually driven out by reinforcements sent by Governor Berkeley.*
   - *Bacon died suddenly of illness, and without his leadership, the rebellion lost momentum.*

- o   *Governor Berkeley regained control and executed many of Bacon's supporters, effectively ending the rebellion.*

5. *Impact and Legacy:*

    - o   *Bacon's Rebellion exposed deep social and economic divisions in colonial Virginia, particularly between wealthy landowners and small farmers.*

    - o   *It led to reforms in Virginia's government, including efforts to address grievances of the western settlers and greater representation for inland areas.*

    - o   *The rebellion also intensified the use of enslaved Africans for labor, as planters sought to reduce reliance on indentured servants who could potentially rebel like Bacon's followers.*

This summary provides an overview of Bacon's Rebellion based on information available in online repositories and historical sources.

Category EVENTS - Timeline of Important Events in 17th Century Virginia

This extract from "The Book" shows the flexibility to identify events as perceived by the author. Graphical icons highlight events pertinent to the Crown, Virginia, Indians, etc., and allow the reader to locate commonalities and pinpoint the source of the information.

Timeline Extract from "The Book"

1618  	By 1618, the Virginia Company was forced to change course again. The Company had not solved the problem of profitability, nor that of settlers' morale.[6] The council in London instructed the Virginia governor to initiate the first representative assembly in the colonies. It was felt that the colonists needed to have some voice in local affairs if order and economic prosperity were to be reestablished in the faltering colony. The legislature lasted until 1624, when a reorganization imposed by the king restored all power to the King's governor. By 1618 the Company had found a way to use its most abundant resource—land—to tempt settlers to pay their own passage from England to the colony and then, after arrival, to pay the Company a quitrent, or fee, to use the land. Still, the Virginia Company and

---

[6] Evolution of the Virginia Colony, 1611-1624, https://www.loc.gov/classroom-materials/united-states-history-primary-source-timeline/colonial-settlement-1600-1763/virginia-colony-1611-1624/ Accessed 05/18/2024.

	the colony it oversaw struggled to survive.[7] After 1618, English settlement significantly encroaches on Indian lands, especially along the Chickahominy and James Rivers. Most of these encroachments are due to private land grants by the Company.
1618	In 1618, Governor Sir George Yeardley founded Flowerdew Hundred, on the south bank of the James. The James River served as a highway of traffic and commerce, much like modern interstates. Early settlements spread along the rivers, sources of reinforcement and communications. Throughout this time, Virginia's population was primarily single males who died young. With few families arriving and high mortality rates from diseases, immigration of new people rather than natural increase accounted for growth.
1619	Heightened efforts at recruiting settlers by Treasurer Sir Edwin Sandys increased the colony's population with offers of land and political authority. Known as particular plantations (called "Hundreds"), these settlements offered incentives to both investors and settlers. In Virginia, new laws passed by the new General Assembly of 1619 also fostered new growth beyond Jamestown to accommodate the increasing arrivals from England. The same year the newly formed Assembly divided Virginia into four counties: James City, Charles City, Henrico and Keghoutan (Elizabeth City), each of which sent representatives to the assembly and formed **county courts.** The beginnings of a legal and political framework were taking hold. New immigrants to the colony would receive 50 acres, as well as an additional 50 for any persons whose passage they financed. This helped increase the flood of immigrants arriving in Virginia. Also fostering the colony's growth was the first substantial influx of unmarried women in 1620. Virginia's population grew rapidly from 1618 until 1622, rising from a few hundred to nearly 1,400 people.[8] Guided by the Company's instructions, the Assembly passes measures to encourage the production of wine, hemp, flax, and, above all, an adequate food supply. The cultivation of tobacco is restricted. Colonists have complained about the high prices charged by the Magazine, and the Assembly limits its profits to 25 percent. Other measures address social behavior, such as idleness, drunkenness, gambling, and **the wearing of apparel beyond one's social station.** Seven private plantations, or "Hundreds", are represented in this first Assembly.[9] Note: In 1619, the first 15 African slaves were brought into Virginia.

---

[7]Virginia Company of London, https://encyclopediavirginia.org/entries/virginia-company-of-london/#:~:text=By%201618%20the%20company%20had,it%20oversaw%20struggled%20to%20survive. Accessed 05/28/2024.

[8] Growth and Settlement Beyond Jamestown, https://www.nps.gov/jame/learn/historyculture/growth-and-settlement-beyond-jamestown.htm Accessed 05/18/2024.

[9]" Thomas Jefferson Papers, 1606 to 1827", Library of Congress, https://www.loc.gov/collections/thomas-jefferson-papers/articles-and-essays/virginia-records-timeline-1553-to-1743/1610-to-1619/ Accessed 1/25/2024.

PROMPT: Create a timeline of events that were important to 17th-century Virginia and explain why they were important

ChatCPT-3.5 as of 06/24/202

Timeline of Important Events in 17th-Century Virginia

1607: Founding of Jamestown

- *Importance: The first permanent English settlement in North America was established by the Virginia Company. It marked the beginning of English colonization in the New World.*

1609-1610: The Starving Time

- *Importance: A period of extreme hardship and famine for Jamestown settlers. This crisis nearly led to the abandonment of the colony but also underscored the importance of supply lines and support from England.*

1612: Introduction of Tobacco Cultivation

- *Importance: John Rolfe successfully cultivates tobacco as a cash crop. Tobacco becomes Virginia's primary export and economic foundation, attracting more settlers and investment.*

1619: First General Assembly

- *Importance: The establishment of the House of Burgesses, the first representative legislative assembly in the American colonies. This event laid the groundwork for democratic governance in the colonies.*

1619: Arrival of the First Enslaved Africans

- *Importance*: Marks the beginning of African slavery in Virginia. Slavery becomes integral to the colony's economy, especially in tobacco farming, and shapes its social and economic structures.

1622: The Indian Massacre

- *Importance*: A coordinated attack by the Powhatan Confederacy that killed a significant portion of the English settlers. This event led to a shift in colonial policies towards Native Americans and fueled further expansion and conflict.

1624: Virginia Becomes a Royal Colony

- *Importance*: The Virginia Company's charter is revoked, and Virginia becomes a royal colony under King James I. This transition shifts control from a private company to the Crown, affecting governance and colonial policy.

1644-1646: Second Anglo-Powhatan War

- *Importance*: Another series of conflicts between English settlers and the Powhatan Confederacy. The war ended with the Treaty of 1646, which confined Native Americans to specific areas and further opened up land for English settlers.

1676: Bacon's Rebellion

- *Importance*: A rebellion led by Nathaniel Bacon against Governor William Berkeley's administration. The uprising was fueled by grievances over land, Native American policy, and lack of protection. It exposed deep tensions between frontier settlers and the colonial government and led to changes in policies *regarding land and labor, including a shift towards a greater reliance on African slaves.*

1693: Founding of the College of William & Mary

- *Importance: Established in Williamsburg, it is the second oldest institution of higher education in America. It played a key role in educating the colony's elite and promoting intellectual growth in the colony.*

Significance of These Events

- *Economic Foundations: The introduction of tobacco cultivation and the reliance on slave labor were pivotal in shaping Virginia's economy and social structures.*
- *Political Development: The establishment of the House of Burgesses and other early governmental institutions set the stage for representative democracy in America.*
- *Conflict and Expansion: Periodic conflicts with Native Americans and internal strife, such as Bacon's Rebellion, highlighted the challenges of colonial expansion and governance, leading to shifts in policies and practices.*
- *Educational and Cultural Growth: The founding of the College of William & Mary contributed to the intellectual and cultural development of the colony.*

These events collectively played a crucial role in the development of Virginia as a powerful and influential English colony, setting precedents and laying the groundwork for future American political, economic, and social systems.

Category PEOPLE - 17th Century First Families of Virginia (FFV)

Extract from "The Book" regarding FFV

17th Century First Families of Virginia (FFV)

The term First Family of Virginia (FFC) did not signify the earliest settlers but rather the early families who had a significant impact on the development of Virginia, including many "cavaliers" who were "second sons" of wealthy families of England who were incented to come to Virginia by Governor Wm Berkely who incented them to establish a group of "elite" settlers who were given large grants of land and used it to develop wealth and an estate of their own.

First Families of Virginia (FFV)
Names PERTINENT TO New Kent COUNTY are highlighted in BOLD

Some notable family names include:

Allerton	Archer	**Bacon**	Baskerville	Belcher
Bentley	**Berkeley**	**Beverley**	Billingsley	Blair
Bland	**Bolling**	Branch	**Braxton**	**Browne**
Buckner	**Burwell**	**Byrd**	Capps	**Carter**
Cary	Chiles	**Christian**	Conway	**Custis**
Dameron	**Dandridge**	Dalton	Eldridge	Fairfax
Farrar	Fielding	Fitzhugh	Gooch	Graves
Hardy	**Harris**	**Harrison**	**Hopkins**	**Jefferson**
Jenings	Kennon	**Lee**	**Madison**	Marshall
Mathews	**West**	Morgan	Nash	Nelson
Norvell	Omohundro	**Page**	Payne	**Randolph**
Robinson	**Rolfe**	Saunders	Selden	**Sharp**
Shifflett	Skillern	**Spencer**	Stagner	Starnes
Stith	Taliaferro	Tayloe	Taylor	Terrell
Waller	Warner	Warren	**Washington**	

Aimy's version:

PROMPT: define the first families of Virginia and explain why certain families were included in this elite group
ChatCPT-3.5 as of 06/24/2024

The First Families of Virginia (FFV) refers to a group of elite families who were among the earliest settlers in the Virginia Colony and rose to prominence and power during the colonial period. These families were distinguished by their wealth, social standing, and influence in the colony's economic, political, and social life.

Definition of the First Families of Virginia

The FFV were typically:

- *Early settlers who arrived in Virginia during the 17th century.*

- *Landowners who acquired large estates, often through headrights and land grants.*
- *Prominent in the colonial government, holding positions such as governors, councilors, and burgesses.*
- *Intermarried with other prominent families, creating a tightly knit aristocratic class.*
- *Involved in the Anglican Church and other social institutions of the colony.*

Reasons for Inclusion in the First Families of Virginia

1. *Early Arrival and Settlement:*
   - *Families who settled in Virginia during the early years of the colony's establishment, typically before 1700, and who helped shape its development.*

2. *Land Ownership and Wealth:*
   - *Large landholders who established plantations and amassed considerable wealth through agriculture, particularly tobacco cultivation.*

3. *Political Influence:*
   - *Individuals who held significant political power and played key roles in the governance of the colony, including serving in the House of Burgesses, the Governor's Council, and other important colonial offices.*

4. *Social Status and Intermarriage:*
   - *Families that maintained their elite status through strategic marriages, often intermarrying with other influential families to consolidate power and wealth.*

5. *Contributions to Colonial Society:*
   - *Contributions to the economic, social, and cultural life of the colony, including involvement in the Anglican Church, education, and other institutions.*

Examples of Prominent FFV

- **Carter Family**: Known for their vast landholdings and political influence, with members like Robert "King" Carter, a wealthy planter and acting Governor of Virginia.
- **Lee Family**: Influential in both colonial and Revolutionary War periods, with notable figures like Richard Henry Lee, a signer of the Declaration of Independence.
- **Randolph Family**: Included influential figures such as Peyton Randolph, the first President of the Continental Congress.
- **Washington Family**: George Washington, the first President of the United States, belonged to this family, which was prominent in both Virginia and national politics.

Significance of the First Families of Virginia (FFV)

The FFV were instrumental in shaping the early history and culture of Virginia. Their economic activities, political leadership, and social customs had a lasting impact on the colony and, later, the state. The legacy of these families continued to influence American history through their descendants, many of whom played prominent roles in the founding and early governance of the United States.

By understanding the criteria and reasons for the inclusion of certain families in the FFV, we can better appreciate their role in the colonial era and their enduring legacy in American history.

Additional request made of Aimy

PROMPT: Create a table of the First Families of Virginia and show what county they lived in

ChatCPT-3.5 as of 06/24/202

Creating a table of the First Families of Virginia (FFV) and the counties they lived in can be challenging, as these families often held land in multiple counties and their estates could span large areas. However, I can provide a list of some notable FFV members along with the primary counties associated with their estates:

Family Name	County/Counties
Berkeley	Charles City, Gloucester
Bolling	Charles City, Chesterfield
Burwell	Gloucester, James City
Carter	Lancaster, Fairfax
Cary	Warwick, Elizabeth City
Custis	Northampton, New Kent
Fairfax	Fairfax, Stafford
Fitzhugh	Stafford, King George
Harrison	Charles City, Prince George
Lee	Westmoreland, Stafford
Lewis	Gloucester, King and Queen
Ludwell	Jamestown, Charles City
Mason	Stafford, Fairfax
Randolph	Henrico, Goochland
Tayloe	Richmond, Essex
Washington	Westmoreland, Fairfax
Wormeley	Middlesex, Gloucester

Notable First Families of Virginia and Their Associated Counties

1. **Berkeley Family**: Charles City, Gloucester
2. **Bolling Family**: Charles City, Chesterfield
3. **Burwell Family**: Gloucester, James City

4. *Carter Family*: Lancaster, Fairfax

5. *Cary Family*: Warwick, Elizabeth City

6. *Custis Family*: Northampton, New Kent

7. *Fairfax Family*: Fairfax, Stafford

8. *Fitzhugh Family*: Stafford, King George

9. *Harrison Family*: Charles City, Prince George

10. *Lee Family*: Westmoreland, Stafford

11. *Lewis Family*: Gloucester, King and Queen

12. *Ludwell Family*: Jamestown, Charles City

13. *Mason Family*: Stafford, Fairfax

14. *Randolph Family*: Henrico, Goochland

15. *Tayloe Family*: Richmond, Essex

16. *Washington Family*: Westmoreland, Fairfax

17. *Wormeley Family*: Middlesex, Gloucester

These families were prominent in the political, economic, and social spheres of colonial Virginia, and many of their descendants played significant roles in American history.

Research on Gideon Macon as presented in "The Book":

Macon, Gideon–Huguenot, Lawyer, Community Leader, Member of House of Burgesses

I discovered that Huguenot, Gideon Macon, was so important to the evolution of New Kent and the role of Frenchmen there that an extra detailed timeline of his life is appropriate. Gideon served in the House of Burgesses from 1796-1705

Macon, Gideon Huguenot	The underwritten are to be transported to Virginia imbarqued in ye Merch Bonaventure in 1634 with James Ricrofte Mr. bound thither have taken ye oath of Allegiance."[10]
Progenitor = William arrived in 1634	Pertinent passenger's name and age on arrival:
Gideon (b.c. 1638 -48, d 4 Mar 1702) HOUSE OF BURGESSES	<table><tr><td>**Mason** *Macon* **William 19** Gideon's father</td><td>Edmonds John 16</td><td>**Fountain** e John 18</td><td>**Hawes** Richard 14 *Progenito r?*</td></tr><tr><td>Hodges John 37.</td><td>**Hughes** Richard 19</td><td>Lewes John 23 ?</td><td>Turner Sara 20</td></tr><tr><td>**Harris** Robert 19</td><td></td><td></td><td></td></tr></table>
Note: There was both Macon and a Mason in early VA and some spelling of Macon as Mason (French soft "c")	[11][12]*Thought to be Gideon Macon's father, William Mason (Anglicized version of Macon) although there was also a valid surname of Mason, Gideon Macon's father, William *Mason* (Anglicized version of Macon) Father Wm Macon. age, 19 in 1634 upon arrival via Bonaventure (Born c. 1615). married Ann Garland

---

[10] Passenger List for Bonadventure. http://www.olivetreegenealogy.com/ships/tova_merchbona1635.shtml Accessed 05/19/2024.

[11] ditto

[12] Macon, Alethea Jane, 1882-, <u>Gideon Macon of Virginia and some of his descendants : allied families.</u> Macon, Ga., Press of the J. W. Burke Co. [1956]. https://babel.hathitrust.org/cgi/pt?id=wu.89061966875&seq=21 Accessed 02/28/2024.

c. 1638	Gideon born to William Macon and Ann Garland Macon about 1638 (1634 + 4 years for 2nd child)
1662	Gideon Macon served as secretary to Gov. Wm Berkely in his second stint as governor (Thereby apprenticing Gideon in the role of attorney.) Gideon = age c. 24
1664 Fellow Huguen Cornelius Dabney 1s land *BOTH become* *Vestryman*	*Fellow future New Kent Parish Vestryman in 1684, Cornelius Dabney, arrived in Virginia by 1664* *(30 years apart from the Macon's father, William)* *Dabney first shows land ownership in 1664:* 406 Cornelius Debarry 1664 200
1664 Woodward Acquired 2100a by Future father-in-law Woodward (Gent)	Gideon's, future father-in-law, and Gentry man, William Woodward father of Martha purchased **2100a in** New Kent: Land grant 23 February 1664. Woodward, William. grantee. 1664 - 02/23 Location: New Kent County. Description: 2100 acres on the **north side of York River**, beginning at the mouth of the creek called John Creek (Jack's?) from thence up the river, including a neck of Sunken ground.[13]. Note: land location was on the north side of York/Pamunkey River as was Cornelius Dabney Observation: This puts Cornelius Dabney, William Woodward, and Gideon Macon as neighbors near the Pamunkey Indian Reservation. ALL three were noted as Indian Interpreters.
1660- 1700s Education to become lawyer was by apprenticeship to attorney	Note about Colonial Virginia lawyers: The English Inns of Court in London had ceased to perform their educational functions in the middle of the seventeenth century.' For the next hundred years or so, there was no formal or organized instruction of the English common law. Lawyers, both barristers and solicitors in England and in America, learned their profession as best they could in unstructured situations. They learned by serving as apprentices or clerks to practicing lawyers, by the independent

---

[13] Source: Land Office Patents No. 5, 1661-1666 (v.1 & 2 p.1-369), p. 509 (Reel 5). https://lva-virginia.libguides.com/land-grants Accessed 02/26/2024.

Likely apprentice to Gov Wm Berkely given that he served as Berkeley's secretary and Berkley had. Been schooled in the law in England.	reading of law books, and by observation in the courtroom itself. In the late seventeenth and early eighteenth centuries, in England and in Virginia, the law was learned primarily through an apprenticeship with a practicing lawyer. The apprentice performed legal and menial chores for his master. One of the more important of these was copying forms, pleadings, and whatever. The apprentice thus did the work of a legal secretary and at the same time gained an intimate knowledge of the contents of the various writs and pleadings. He carried his master's books and notes into court and, of course, remained in court to observe the legal proceedings there and his master's handling of the case. He had the use of his master's law library, and the master had an obligation to teach his apprentice the art of practicing law.[14]
1671-81	Court Records of York County showing that Gideon Macon was an attorney-at-law in that county as early as 1671 and for a decade thereafter. (If born in 1638, he would have been age 29.)
1672 + Attorney in York County To the Gentry family of Richard Major Article notes Gideon was an Indian Interpreter (as was Cornelius Dabney)	GIDEON MACON and subsequently his descendants were so closely identified with the Major family as to merit a word of special mention, and a brief notice of them is in consequence appended. GIDEON MACON born circa 1650, was living in York county, an attorney at law, prior to 1672. He was by tradition at one time an Indian interpreter and secretary to Sir William Berkeley. He was named under-sheriff of York, under Daniel Wild, his brother-in-law, 3 April 1672, Richard James being his security. His name thereafter frequently figures in the York records for the next decade; he lived for a while in James City county, and was a vestryman of Bruton parish in 1678; but about 1682 he removed to New Kent, where he made his permanent home. St. Peter's parish records show that Gideon Macon was vestryman and churchwarden before 1684 and until his death.[15] Macon's tenure as secretary to the Governor came at the end of Governor Berkeley's second administration (1660–1677), and Macon served as his secretary in 1677. (*after Bacon's rebellion*)[16]

---

[14]The History of Legal Education in Virginia,

https://scholarship.law.wm.edu/cgi/viewcontent.cgi?article=1007&context=history Accessed 05/21/2024.

[15] Macon of New Kent,

https://archive.org/details/majorstheirmarri00cabe/page/n98/mode/1up?view=theater&q=macon Accessed 05/21/2024.

[16]Gideon Macon, https://en.wikipedia.org/wiki/Gideon_Macon Accessed 02/18/2024.

1677	Father, William Macon, also owned a tavern house in James City. Following Bacon's Rebellion, (1676) he leased the tavern house to the Colonial Government of Virginia because its office buildings had been burned down during the rebellion. Upon William Macon's death, income from the building was paid to his widow, Ann (Garland) Macon. (on record:"12,000 pounds of tobacco to use her house for meetings") Upon her death in 1699, her will left items to son Gideon Macon and his children. *Note: Her will provides additional evidence as proof that Ann (Garland) Macon was the mother of Gideon Macon.*
1678 Of York County Serving as attorney to widow of the Major family	William Major had married, circa 1665, Elizabeth, daughter of Colonel Lemuel Mason of Norfolk county. She survived her husband, and was appointed his administratrix, 24 April 1678, giving bond with her attorney, Gideon Macon, for £500, as guardian to her three sons. A note as to Gideon Macon is given on page 50. KNOW ALL MEN by these presents that wee, ELIZABETH MAJOR widdow, and GIDEON MACON, both of Yorke County, are holden & firmly bound unto ye Worsh'p'll his Ma'ties Justices of the Peace for Yorke County in ye sum of five hundred pound sterl, money of England, to be paid upon demand; to the w'ch payment, well and truely to be made, wee bind ourselves joyntly and sevearlly our and either of our heirs, Exec'rs & Adm'rs firmly by these presents. Witness our hands and seles, dated in Virginia, ye 24th of Aprilis 1678.
1678 First mention as Vestryman	Served as Church Warden in in Burton parish of Middle Plantation. Bruton Parish, which had been created in 1674 by uniting Marston Parish of York County and Middletown Parish* of James City County. The records of Bruton Parish show that on 14 Nov. 1648 he, with William Aylett, John Page, Phillip Ludwell, et al, contributed liberally toward the building of "a Brick Church on the Middle Plantation for ye said Parish." This church, dedicated on Epiphany 1684 by the Rev. Rowland Jones, later became the foundation of the New Church completed in 1715. Repaired, remodeled, and restored throughout the years, New Church, now known as Bruton Parish Church, still stands on the Duke of Gloucester Street in Williamsburg — one of the most historic edifices in all America. On one of its pews is a brass tablet in memory of Gideon

Macon, one of the first Vestrymen of Bruton Parish.[17] pon his removal to New Kent County about 1680, Gideon Macon established his home on Macon's Island in the Pamunkey River, near his large plantation on the south bank of that river.

Land patents by him include extensive acreage, not only in New Kent, but also in Henrico and King and Queen Counties. About this time, he was married to Martha Woodward of King William County. Her father was William Woodward who, having won the good will of the Pamunkey Indians, was invited by their Queen, Cocka Coeste, to take up 2,000 acres of land among them; this, he accordingly did.

Note: Bruton Parish was formed in 1674 when Marston Parish (formed in 1654) in York County merged with Middletown Parish. The first vestrymen for Bruton Parish, named at its creation in 1674, were Col. Thomas Ballard Sr., Daniel Parke, Col. John Page, James Besouth, Robert Cobbs, James Bray, Capt. Philip Chesley and William Aylett.[8]

--Gideon donated 5 lbs. along with others toward build a brick church in 1678. Burton parish was near Williamsburg and Gideon was recognized for his contribution to Burton. He was an early Vestryman in Bruton Parish, where a brass tablet to his memory still marks a pew in the church.

---

[17]Gideon Macon of Virginia and some of his descendants. Allied families,

https://archive.org/stream/gideonmaconofvir00maco/gideonmaconofvir00maco_djvu.txt

Accessed 5/3/2024.

> Wee, the subscribers, do hereby oblige ourselves, our heires, and Executors, and Administrators, to pay each of us five pounds Sterling to the Vestry, upon demand, towards ye building of A Brick Church, on ye Middle Plantation, for ye said Parish, as witness our hands this 14th of November, 1678.
>
> Witness
>
> Abraham Vinckler,
> Richard Curteen.
>
> James Besouth,   Martin Gardner,
> Wm. Aylett,   Gideon Macon,
> Robert Cobb,   Tho. Taylor,
> Robert Spring,   Christo Pearson."
>
> On the 5th June, 1679, a full description of the Church to be built is given, together with articles of agreement between the Vestry and George Marable, the contractor of the work, which was to cost £350 sterling.[18]

Note on timing of the French in New Kent:

Huguenot Cornelius Dabney, first land acquisition in 1664 in New Kent in 1664, Vestry man of St. Peter's parish in 1684

Huguenot, Gideon Macon, first mention and lawyer in York County in 1677 and Secretary to Gov. Wm Berkeley in 1677, leadership position in New Kent 1684

Huguenot Robert DePriest bought land in New Kent in 1689

Manakintown Huguenots came later in 1700

Huguenot Jerome/Jeremiah Dumas arrived with first batch of Manakintown Huguenots in 1700

Observation: It is significant that Gideon had gained the status to become a Church Warden for Burton parish after serving as an attorney in York Count before moving to New Kent in 1680. It appears his social status was the result of his legal work and his association with Governor Wm Berkeley rather than as huge landowner in New Kent. His political clout aided his first election to the House of Burgesses in 1693.

Observation:

---

[18] The Record of Burton Parish Church by Goodwin, https://tile.loc.gov/storage-services/public/gdcmassbookdig/historicalsketch01good/historicalsketch01good.pdf Accessed 05/20/2024.

	Having a French Huguenot serve as a Vestryman was highly unusual for 17th Century Virginia and may have been a factor of why other early Huguenots found in New Kent attractive including Robert DePriest. Even more significant is that Gideon Macon was elected to the House of Burgesses in the 17th Century even though a Frenchman. Note: map of James City, York and Williamsburg areas near each other before Gideon's move further westward to New Kent.
1680	Gideon Macon moved to New Kent County about 1680 and established his home on Macon's Island. This is not a true island in the Pamunkey River except during times of high water but is connected by an isthmus crossing Macon's Creek during times of low water which is most of the time.
Land acquired by Gideon 1698. 148a Henrico (3 headrights) 1698 545a in New Kent (11 headrights) 1701. 72a+415a. (13 Headrights In King & Queen	of at least equal responsibility, since he was chosen to represent New Kent in the Virginia House of Burgesses for the sessions beginning 10 October 1693 and 24 September 1696. Land-patents by Gideon Macon include grants of 148 acres in Henrico County, 15 October 1698, due for the transportation of three persons; 545 acres in New Kent, 7 November 1700, for the transportation of eleven; and two grants in King and Queen, 25 April 1701, of 172 and 425 acres respectively, for the transportation of thirteen persons.
1681 Marriage	Gideon I married his wife, Martha Woodward in early 1681. (One year after moving to New Kent) would have been about age 22 when he married Martha Woodward.

1682 Firstborn SON Gideon II born	1682. Gideon and Martha Macon had Gideon Jr., their first child born in 1682 according to the St. Peters parish records. It was very normal to have a child in the first year of marriage.
1684.	In his new home in New Kent, Gideon Macon continued his activity in the Church of England. **The first entry in the Vestry Book of St. Peter's Parish** in that county was in "**1684,** Anno Regis 35th," when the Rev. Mr. Carr was Rector and <u>Gideon Macon, Church Warden</u>. In 1684 it appears that after his father, William Macon, died, a Mrs. Ann Macon (presumably his widow) was granted an "allowance of 12,000 pounds of Tobacco for use of her House as Committee Chambers, Assembly Room, Clerk's office, the Council Chamber, etc." This house is assumed to be on a plantation on Macon Island going by the name of Mount Prospect on Macon Island, in New Kent County.
1687	1687 St. Peters of New Kent, Church Leaders: Note: Indian Interpreter Cornelius Dabney became church leader along with fellow Huguenot Gideon Macon.

John Page	**Cornelius Dabney**	**Gideon Macon**
Matthew Page	Stephen Tarleton	Henry Wyatt
George Smith	John Parks	Thomas Mitchell
David Crawford	William Peasley	John Roper
William Bassett		

1693, 1696-'97, 1698, 1699, and 1700-'02	The Journals of the Virginia House of Burgesses show that Gideon Macon represented New Kent County in that body for the sessions, 1693, 1696-'97, 1698, 1699, and 1700-'02, his colleague from that county for most of the time being William Bassett.
HOUSE OF BURGESSES	
1694	Land grant 20 April 1694. 1694 - 0420 : 155 acres it being the **island** on the northeast side of the main run of Chickahominy Swamp; at the Wading Place near Meradays plantation.
Land grants 1698-1701	Land Acquisition via headrights 1698, 1700, and 1701 148a for transportation of of 3, then 545a for 11, and more 425+a for 13

15 October 1698 in Henrico	**148 acres in Henrico County, 15 October 1698, due for the transportation of three persons; 545 acres in New Kent, 7 November 1700, for the transportation of eleven; and two grants in King and Queen, 25 April 1701, of 172 and 425 acres respectively, for the transportation of thirteen persons.**
1699 Gideon's mother, Ann names Gideon in her will	Anne (Ann Garland) Macon's will of 1699-1700. (widow of Gideon's father, Wm Macon) "Anne Macon of St. Botolph, Algate, London, widow. Will dated 7 September 1699; proved 3 August 1700". "To Mr. Gideon Macon now living in Virginia and to his wife to each of them a ring of 20s apiece. To Gideon Macon, his son, my silver tankard & c. To Ann Macon, daughter of Gideon Macon the elder my silver porringer. To Martha my six silver spoons. To Mary Elwenn, spinster, all my wearing linen and my best hood …
1700	He is known to have made on 10 Oct. 1700 a will, which was probated in proper form, his wife Martha being named executrix; (Martha Woodward Macon)
1700 Gideon Sr abandoned land in Henrico and was re-patented to the son Wm Major *(son of Richard Major?)*	**York deceased." The younger William Major patented 150 acres in New Kent county, 7 November 1700, (the land being a tract deserted by Gideon Macon), as due for the transpor-** [19] Note: 148-150a in Henrico deserted by Gideon and re-patented by younger William Major. Gideon had served as lawyer to the parents of younger Wm Major.
1701 Gideon Sr acquired more land near the Pamunkey Indian Reservation before his death in 1702	April 25, 1701, Land Patent., "King and Queen County, 425ac. Beginning g. &c. In Pampatike swamp. Adjoining Tho. Spencer's land. North & c. crossing John's creek". Patent 9, page 354. (*Note: this land was on north side of Pamunkey River on the Pamunkey neck near the Pamunkey Indian Reservation as was the land of Cornelius Dabney)* Another patent on the same day and year, April 25, 1701.Land Patent. "King

---

[19]The Majors and Their Families,

https://archive.org/details/majorstheirmarri00cabe/page/n77/mode/1up?view=theater&q=macon Accessed 02/17/2024.

	and Queen County, 172ac., In Pamunkey neck, on the East side of Pampatike swamp. Beginning g. & c. in the head line of his 425ac. Parcel of Pullam's patent". Patent 9, page 354. *Note: these land patents were in King and Queen County which had been formed from New Kent County to the North.*

1701
 	
Children of Gideon and Martha (Woodward Wild) named in list:
 	
Note: Marriages Anne married James Christian
Martha m. Orlando Jones
Wm b. 1693 m. Mary Hartwell
	1701, a vestry meeting being held on that date at his home, and was "lately decest" 4 March 1702, when his successor as vestryman was elected.
	    Gideon Macon and his wife, Martha Wild, had issue:
	    I. GIDEON MACON, born 20 June 1682.
	    II. ANNE MACON, born 15 December 1685, living in 1728, who married James Christian of Charles City county.
	    III. MARTHA MACON, born 1687, who married Orlando Jones of King William county.
	    IV. WILLIAM MACON, born 12 November 1693, who married Mary, daughter of William Hartwell.
	    V. JOHN MACON, born 17 December 1695, living 1729 in Goochland county, who had with other issue a son Henry Macon.
	    VI. JAMES MACON, born 28 October 1701, who married Elizabeth, daughter of Augustine Moore, and had, with other issue, a daughter, Mary Macon, who married William Aylett.

1701.- 1702	He continued as an official of the parish until his death. On 8 Dec. 1701, A Vestry meeting was held at his home; at the next meeting held 4 Mar. 1702, he was recorded as "lately deceased" and Henry Childs was elected to succeed him.
1702	Martha, Widow of Gideon Macon was paid 12,000 pounds of tobacco for the use of her home for county/parish business.
1703	Martha remarried to Nathaniel West and had daughter Unity West

	Gideon Macon's widow had re-married by 24 June 1703, on which date there was a suit in York between Nathan West and Martha, his wife, the relict and executrix of Gideon Macon, and Richard Packe of London. By this second marriage with Nathaniel West, she had issue: Unity West, who married William Dandridge, and had: Nathaniel West Dandridge, who married and left issue by Dorothea Spotswood. The wife of Gideon Macon married, third, ——— Bigger.
1704	Name on 1704 New Kent quit rents list : Meacon [Macon], Gideon, 270acres (had to be Gideon Jr., as Gideon Sr died in 1702) Name on processioning of 1689 = Gideon MACON had to be Gideon Sr. The last record of Gideon Macon Jr. that has been found is that of a conveyance to Thomas Mimms of "74a of land in Chickahominy Swamp, part of a tract granted to my father in 1698," dated 28 Apr. 1704. (Henrico Co. Book of Deeds, 1700- 1704, p. 405). *Conflict: 148 a in Henrico, deserted by Gideon Sr was re-patented to young Wm Major; could be that Gideon Jr. sold land to Mims which he thought was still owned by his father Gideon Sr.*
1716 Gideon was ancestor to first lady, Martha Washington	compare the *William and Mary College Quarterly*, Volumes VI, X, XII, and XIV. Of his daughters, Martha Macon, born in 1687, died 4 May 1716, married Orlando Jones (who survived her, and married, second, Mary, daughter of James Williams), and had issue: Lane Jones; and Frances Jones, who married Colonel John Dandridge, and was the mother of Martha Dandridge, who married, first, John Custis, and, second, George Washington.

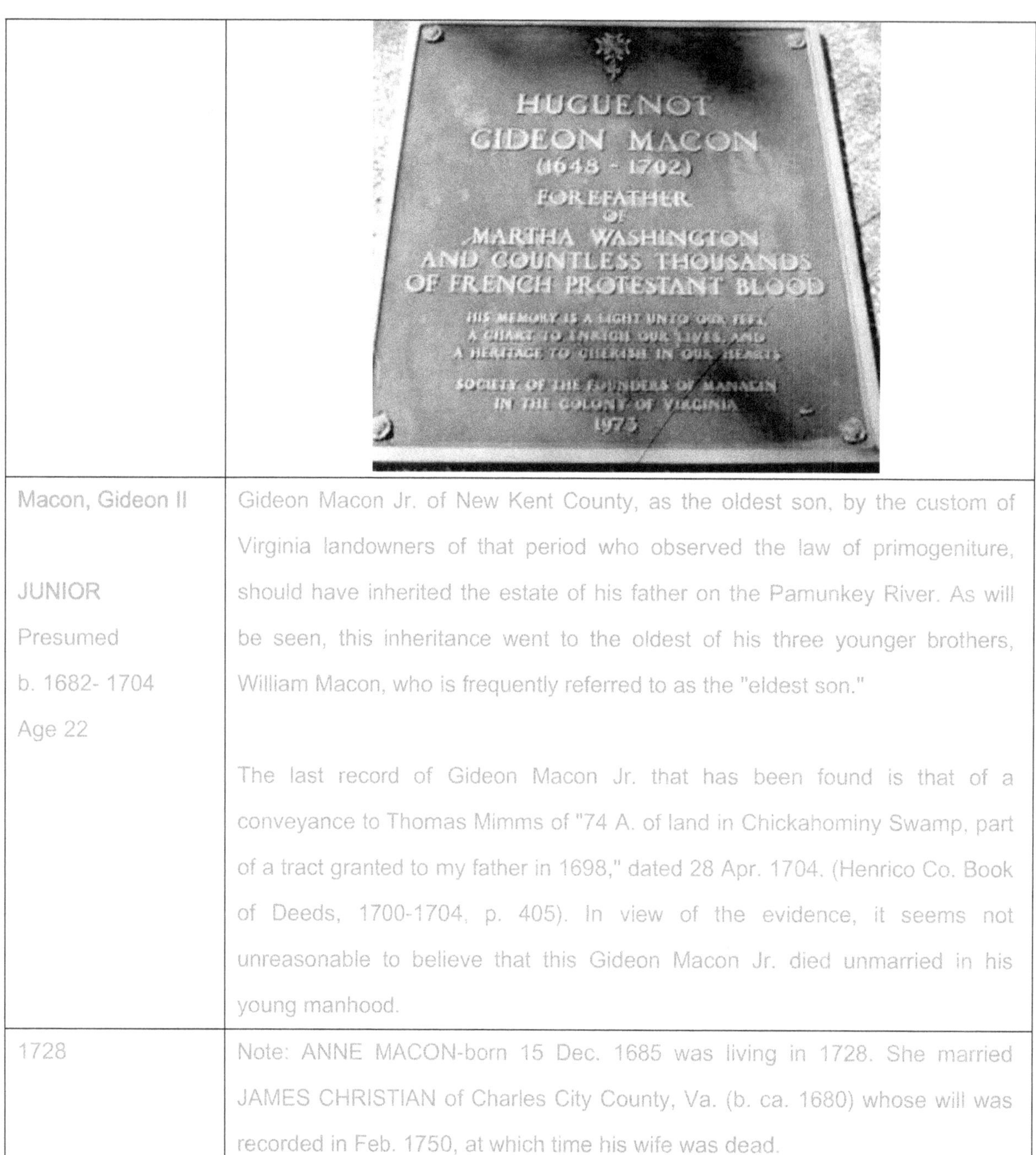	
Macon, Gideon II JUNIOR Presumed b. 1682- 1704 Age 22	Gideon Macon Jr. of New Kent County, as the oldest son, by the custom of Virginia landowners of that period who observed the law of primogeniture, should have inherited the estate of his father on the Pamunkey River. As will be seen, this inheritance went to the oldest of his three younger brothers, William Macon, who is frequently referred to as the "eldest son." The last record of Gideon Macon Jr. that has been found is that of a conveyance to Thomas Mimms of "74 A. of land in Chickahominy Swamp, part of a tract granted to my father in 1698," dated 28 Apr. 1704. (Henrico Co. Book of Deeds, 1700-1704, p. 405). In view of the evidence, it seems not unreasonable to believe that this Gideon Macon Jr. died unmarried in his young manhood.
1728	Note: ANNE MACON-born 15 Dec. 1685 was living in 1728. She married JAMES CHRISTIAN of Charles City County, Va. (b. ca. 1680) whose will was recorded in Feb. 1750, at which time his wife was dead.

Aimy's take on Gideon Macon

Prompt: Tell me everything you know about Huguenot Gideon Macon of 17th-century Virginia

ChatCPT-3.5 06/25/2024

Gideon Macon, a notable Huguenot figure in 17th-century Virginia, played a significant role in the colony's political, religious, and social spheres. Here is a detailed account of his life and contributions:

Early Life and Background

- *Birth and Origins*: Gideon Macon was born around 1648. Although some sources suggest he may have been born in England, there is speculation that he could have been of Huguenot descent, indicating he might have had French Protestant ancestry.
- *Migration to Virginia*: Macon migrated to Virginia in the latter part of the 17th century. The exact date of his arrival is uncertain, but it is believed to be in the late 1660s or early 1670s. The migration of Huguenots to the New World was often driven by religious persecution in France following the revocation of the Edict of Nantes in 1685, although Macon's arrival predated this event.

Career and Contributions

- *Planter and Landowner*: Gideon Macon became a prosperous planter in Virginia, acquiring significant tracts of land. He was heavily involved in the cultivation of tobacco, which was the primary cash crop of the colony.
- *Political and Civic Involvement*:
  - *House of Burgesses*: Macon served as a member of the House of Burgesses, Virginia's legislative assembly. His role in the House of Burgesses demonstrated his influence and leadership within the colony.
  - *Clerk of the Council*: He also served as the Clerk of the Council, an important administrative position that further underscored his prominence in colonial governance.
  - *Vestryman*: Macon was an active member of the vestry of Bruton Parish Church in Williamsburg, reflecting his significant role in the local Anglican Church and his contributions to community and religious life.

Personal Life

- *Marriage and Family*:

- o ***First Marriage***: Gideon Macon married Martha Woodward, the daughter of William Woodward, a prominent landowner and trader. This marriage alliance helped to solidify Macon's social and economic standing in Virginia.
- o ***Children***: The couple had several children, including Martha Macon, who later married Orlando Jones. This connection made Gideon Macon the great-grandfather of Martha Washington, the wife of George Washington.
- o ***Second Marriage***: After the death of his first wife, Macon remarried. His second wife was Sarah Jones, further extending his familial and social network.

Legacy

- ***Macon Family***: The Macon family became influential in both Virginia and broader American history. A notable descendant is Nathaniel Macon, who served as Speaker of the U.S. House of Representatives and a U.S. Senator from North Carolina.
- ***Land and Estate***: Gideon Macon's extensive landholdings and management practices contributed to the wealth and status of his descendants, securing their position in Virginian society.
- ***Bruton Parish Church***: Macon's involvement in Bruton Parish Church left a lasting mark in the Williamsburg area, with the church remaining an important historical and cultural landmark.

Death

- ***Passing***: Gideon Macon died in 1702 in New Kent County, Virginia. His will and estate records provide valuable insights into his wealth, property, and social standing at the time of his death.

The exact same prompt given to **Chat GPT-4.0** reads a bit differently:

ChatGPT-4.0

Gideon Macon (sometimes spelled Mason) was a prominent Huguenot who emigrated from France to Virginia in the 17th century. He is noted for his role as a settler and his contributions to the early development of the colony. While specific records about his early life in France are scarce, his impact in Virginia is better documented. Here are some key details about Gideon Macon:

1. ***Background and Immigration:*** *Gideon Macon was born in France, and like many Huguenots of the time, he fled to escape religious persecution after the revocation of the Edict of Nantes in 1685. This edict had previously provided some protections for Protestants in Catholic-majority France.*

2. ***Settlement in Virginia:*** *Gideon Macon settled in New Kent County, Virginia, an area that became a significant center for Huguenot immigrants. New Kent County and its environs offered a welcoming environment for Huguenots, who were known for their skills in agriculture, craftsmanship, and trade.*

3. ***Contributions and Influence:*** *Macon quickly adapted to life in Virginia and became a successful planter and landowner. He was involved in the local governance and community affairs, which was typical for a man of his standing in the colony.*

4. ***Family and Legacy:*** *Gideon Macon married Martha Woodward, and together they had several children. His descendants, including Nathaniel Macon, became influential in American politics and society. Nathaniel Macon, in particular, served as a U.S. Senator and as Speaker of the U.S. House of Representatives.*

5. ***Religious Impact:*** *Although specific details about Gideon Macon's religious activities are not extensively documented, like many Huguenots, he likely continued to practice his Protestant faith in Virginia. The Huguenots had a*

significant religious influence in the region, contributing to the growth of Protestant denominations such as the Anglican and Presbyterian churches.

6. ***Death and Legacy:*** *Gideon Macon died in 1702 in Virginia. His legacy includes not only his immediate family's contributions to American society but also his role as part of the larger Huguenot influence on early American colonial culture and development.*

Gideon Macon is remembered as a symbol of the resilience and entrepreneurial spirit of the Huguenot refugees who helped shape the early American colonies. His descendants and the broader Huguenot community continue to celebrate this heritage.

Accuracy of Content

REMINDER: ChatGPT will always provide a response that typically sounds right, but it needs to be verified before assuming it is true.

Note that Aimy assumes the question is about Gideon Macon, as he is the topic of the previous conversation.

PROMPT: Can AI cite sources of facts
ChatCPT-3.5 06/25/2024

Yes, I can certainly provide sources for the information on Gideon Macon. Here are some references to support the facts mentioned:

Early Life and Background

- ***Birth and Origins****: Information on Gideon Macon's birth and potential Huguenot descent is often sourced from genealogical records and historical texts such as "The Huguenots in America: A Refugee People in New World Society" by Jon Butler.*

Career and Contributions

- *Planter and Landowner*: The economic activities of Gideon Macon, including his role as a planter, are documented in historical records of land grants and economic activities in colonial Virginia.
- *Political and Civic Involvement*:
  - *House of Burgesses*: Macon's service in the House of Burgesses is recorded in the "Journals of the House of Burgesses of Virginia."
  - *Clerk of the Council*: His role as Clerk of the Council can be found in administrative records of the Virginia Colony.
  - *Vestryman*: His involvement with Bruton Parish Church is detailed in church records and historical accounts such as "Colonial Churches of Virginia" by Edmund S. Morgan.

Personal Life

- *Marriage and Family*:
  - *First Marriage and Children*: Genealogical records, such as those found on sites like Ancestry.com, provide information about Macon's marriage to Martha Woodward and their descendants.
  - *Second Marriage*: Details of his second marriage can also be found in genealogical sources and family histories.

Legacy

- *Macon Family*: The influence of the Macon family is documented in various historical and biographical works, including "Nathaniel Macon of North Carolina" by William E. Dodd.
- *Land and Estate*: Records of Macon's landholdings and estate are available in colonial Virginia land grant documents and wills.
- *Bruton Parish Church*: The history of Bruton Parish Church, including Macon's involvement, is covered in church archives and local historical studies.

Death

- ***Passing***: Gideon Macon's death and will are documented in probate records and genealogical sources.

Historical Significance

- ***General Context***: The broader context of Huguenot migration and their impact on American society can be found in historical studies such as "The Huguenot Settlements in Virginia" by R.A. Brock and "The Huguenots of Colonial South Carolina" by Arthur Henry Hirsch.

By referring to these sources, you can verify the information and gain a deeper understanding of Gideon Macon's life and legacy in 17th-century Virginia.

More detail regarding sources sites **per ChatGPT-4.0 as** of 06/26/2024
PROMPT: can AI cite sources of facts about Huguenot Gideon Macon of 17th century Virginia   ChatGPT-4.0

Yes, AI can cite sources for facts about historical figures like Gideon Macon, a Huguenot in 17th-century Virginia. Here is an example of how it can be done:

Primary Sources: These include original documents such as wills, land grants, and court records. For example, Gideon Macon's land patents or his will might be found in colonial Virginia archives.

Secondary Sources: These are works of historians or scholars who have studied the primary sources. An example would be the book Huguenot Emigration to Virginia by R. A. Brock.

Tertiary Sources: These include encyclopedias and databases summarizing historical data. Examples include entries in the Encyclopedia Virginia or genealogical websites like Ancestry.com.

Sample Citations

Primary Source:

Macon, Gideon. Will of Gideon Macon. Colonial Wills of Henrico County, Virginia, 17th Century. Virginia Colonial Archives.

Secondary Source:

Brock, R. A. Huguenot Emigration to Virginia. The Genealogical Publishing Company, 1886.

Tertiary Source:

"Gideon Macon." Encyclopedia Virginia. Virginia Foundation for the Humanities, 2010.

If you need more specific sources or detailed information, please let me know!

Since Aimy asked me if I needed more, I added this question to our chat:

PROMPT: I would like more specific resources you used to research Gideon Macon

ChatGPT-4.0

Searched 6 sites

Gideon Macon, a notable figure in 17th-century Virginia, was a French Huguenot who emigrated to the American colonies. His journey likely began in England, where the Macon family had settled following their departure from France, possibly due to the St. Bartholomew's Day Massacre or the Huguenot persecutions preceding the Edict of Nantes in 1598 (Jamestowne Society) (FamilySearch).

Macon arrived in Virginia before 1670 and became an influential attorney in York County by 1671. He served as secretary to Governor Sir William Berkeley during Berkeley's second administration (1660-1677). In 1680, he moved to New Kent County and established his estate, Mount Prospect Plantation, on Macon's Island along the Pamunkey River. That same year, he married Martha Woodward, the daughter of William Woodward, an interpreter for the Pamunkey tribe(Wikipedia) (Jamestowne Society).

Gideon Macon held several significant positions throughout his life. He was a vestryman and churchwarden at Bruton Parish Church and St. Peter's Parish, respectively. In 1693, and from 1696 to 1702, he served as a member of the House of Burgesses, representing New Kent County. He was also the commander-in-chief of the New Kent County Militia, earning the title of Colonel (Wikipedia) (Jamestowne Society) (WikiTree.com).

Upon his death in 1702, Gideon Macon's legacy continued through his children and grandchildren, notably through his great-granddaughter, Martha Dandridge, who became the wife of George Washington (Wikipedia).

Category METHODs: Discovering New Information In Old Data

Having delved into large quantities of old, "dead" records, I found I kept returning to certain methods to help me dig for the truth. One of my favorite source documents is the Parish Records of St. Peter's/Paul's of New Kent County. Time-consuming trial and error is often used when trying to discover new information from old data.

Extract from "The Book"

Compare Changes in Similar Data Collections Over Time
Below is a chart I built to compare processioning records of the same Parish over a different block of time used to help determine the spelling of Surnames -specifically Comparing Surname Spelling From the 1704 Tax List, 1689 Processions List, And 1677 Blissland Rebel Signers in the area of New Kent County, Virginia

This chart begins with all the names in New Kent in the 1704 quit rents list and compares them to those who were also in the 1689 Processing of St. Peters Parish and those who signed as dissenters in the 1677 formal grievances to the Crown.

Note: The names greyed out in the table are deemed not pertinent to this study but serve to demonstrate the exceptionally high turnover of landowners.

Comparison Chart of New Kent County Landowners by Years 1677, 1689, and 1704

Name Spelling in 1704 Base year	Acreage in year 1704	Name spelling in 1689 *15 years earlier*	1677 Signer *27 years earlier*	Comment
Aldridge, Jn o	250	Jno. Aldridge		John Aldridge Deceased April 16, 1720.
Alex. [Alexander] Abraham -	100			
Alford, John	**240**	Alford		

Allen, Reynold	205	**Renall** Allen		*- named son Renall would be to honor a friend/neighbor with surname Renall.* **VERY likely French**
Allen, Daniel -	250	Ruth Allen		*Ruth,= likely Richard's sister who had to be unmarried at time of processioning to be listed as a female. widow of Daniel Allen would likely be listed as "Widow Allen"*
Allen, Richard -	550	Rich. **Allen**		
Allen, Rob t -	100			
Allen, Sam ll -	150			
Allvis, George -	325			
Amos, Nich o -	50			
Amoss, Fran -	100			
Anderson, David -	300			
Anderson, Jn o -	100	Jno. Andrenson		
Anderson, John -	100	Jno. Andrewson		son of Robert and Mary
Anderson, Rich d -	200			
Anderson, Rob t -	**700**	Rob't **Andrewson**	1677	Gentry who signed Blisland list of grievances addressed to the King
Anderson, Robt. -	**900**			ditto
Anthony, Mark -	190			
Arise, Marg t -	200			
Aron, Josiah -	200			
Ashcroft, Tho. -	180			
Ashley, Charles -	100			
Atkinson, Jn - likely son of Wm Atkinson list earlier in 1689	300	Wm. Atkinson		**1684** To Wm. Atkinson for Parish Ferry. - 1687 It is ordered that **Will. Atkinson** do Levie ye Ferry from ye nth of December next, for the ensuing year, & to be allowed eight hundred of Tob. & Cs'k.
Austin -	245			
Austin, James -	**700**	James Austin	**1677**	James Austin "Middling" Gentry who signed Blisland list of grievances addressed to the King
Austin, Rich d	50			

Bad, Sam ll -	150			
Baker, Christo	100	Chris. Baker		1691: To **Mr.** Xtoph'e Baker for keeping John Hannewell one mon. & burying him 00150
Baker, Jn o -	130			
Baker, Rich d -	80			
Ball, David -	200			Ball or Bell?
Banks, Andrew -	50			
Barbar, Tho. -	500			
Barker, Chas. -	100			
Barnhowes, Rich d ***Barnhouse-***	1600		1677	**NICHOLAS** BARNHOUSE Gentry who signed Blisland list of grievances addressed to the King

Barrett, Christ o -	60		1677	
Bassett, Tho. -	350			
Bassett, Wm. -	550	**Mr.** Wm Bassett		Wm Bassett was very large land holder in New Kent by 1704
Bassett, Wm. Esqr.	**4100**	Wm. Bassett		
Bassett, Wm., Esqr. -	**1250**			
Bates, Edw d -	50			
Baughan, Jn o -	100	Jno. Baughn	1677	
Baughan, Jn o Jun r -	300			
Baughan, Joseph -	100		1677	
Baughtwright [Boatwright], Jn	250			
Baxter, James -	90			
Bayley, Jno. -	80			
Bear, Peter -	100			
Beare, Joseph -	150			
Bearne, Henry -	50			
Beck, Wm. -	433			
Beck, Wm. Mr. -	200			
Blackburn, Rowland -	700			Rowland Blackbourn Departed this Life 81" ye 20th, 1713.
Blackwell, James -	950	James Blackwell	1677	**Rbt** Blackwell to replace James Blackwell, deceased St. Pauls Vestry 1705 Gentry who signed Blisland list of grievances addressed to the King
Blackwell, James, Jun r -	200			James Blackwell Ju' & Mary Glenn marr'^ the 18 Apr. 1699.
Blalock, Jn o -	492			
Bostock, Jn o -	100	**Chas** Bostick	1677 **Bostwick**	**Charles** Bostock dyed ye 4 January, 1700-1. Mary Bostrik Departed this Life December ye 7th, 1709.
Bostock, Wm. -	80			
Bourn, Wm. -	140			
Bow, Henry -	200			
Bowles, John -	500			
Bradbury, Geo. -	100			
Bradingham, Rob t	150			
Bradley, Tho. -	255			
Bray, Sarah -	**790**			Mad'm Sarah Bray Departed this life 8b' ye 18th, 1716. wife of Col• David Bray
Breeding [Breeden], John -	300			
Brewer, Mary -	100			
Brooks, Rich d -	85	**Jer.** Brooke Related?		Rich **Brooker** Dyed Decemb' ye 10th, 1723.

Brooks, Rob t -	45			
Brothers, Jn o -	200			
Brown, Jn o -	100	Jno. Browne		*John Brown* (no "E") neighbor of DePriest in 1689 J Brown Departed this Life Febry: ye 10th, 1709. Thom. Browne deceased ye 17 d. of Decem', 1687. *(related?)*
Bryan, Charles -	100	Chas. Bryan		
Bugg, Sam ll -	60			Samuel Buggs Departed this Life 7'" ye 13th, 1716 Deborah ye wife of Sam11 Bugg Departed this Life ye 14th of X"', 1715.
Bulkley, Benj a -	200			
Bullock, Edw d -	450			
Bullock, Rich d	450	Richard Bollork Sen.& Jr		Bullock
Bumpass, [Bumpas] Rob t	100			
Buncle, John -	100			
Burkett, Tho. -	41			
Burly, Jn o -	225			
Burnell [Burwell] Mary, Mrs.	2750			
Burnell, Edw d -	200			
Burnett, John -	150			
Burwell, Lewis -	200			
Butts, Alice -	150	Mrs.Botts		M" Alice Butts Departed this Life July ye 20th, 171S. (wife of."of M' Tho. Butts")

Cambo, Rich d	80			
Carley, Rich d –	80	Rich.d Cawdry Corley	1677	Rich **CORLEY** in 1677
Carlton, Wm. -	140			
Case, Hugh -	100			
Chambers, Edw d -	235			
Chambers, George -	100			
Chandler, Frances -	150			
Chandler, Rob t -	160	Rob't Chandler		
Chandler, Wm. -	300			
Chesley, Wm. -	500			
Chiles, Henry -	700	Hen. Chilloe		
Clarkson, David -	200	David Clarkston		David Clarkson Departed this Life april 15, 1720. Peter Clarkson Departed this Life ye 30th day of December 17 I 1. Eliz: Clarkson Deceased april 17, 1720.
Clerk, Christ o -	300			
Clerk, Edw d -	282			
Clopton, Wm. -	**454**			**Different person than Clayton**
Clough, Capt.	80			

Name	Acres	Alt. Name	Year	Notes
[George?] Cocker, Wm. -	1000			
Collett, Tho. -	100			
Colum, Rich d -	130			
Cook, Abraham -	200			
Cordey, Tho. -	150			
Cos, Wm. – *Cox?*	350	Will. Cox		*same person?*
Cotrell, Rich d -	200			Richard Cotterell Departed this Life March ye 16th, 1715. Richard Cotterell Jun' Departed this Life 81" 13th, 1715. Gilbert Cotterell Dyed ye 25 of b'", 1724. W'" Cotterell Died Febry 13th, 1725-6. Thomas Cotterell Departed this Life april ye 22d, 1718.
Crawford, David, Jr.	400	**Jno. Crawford**		David Jr. in 1704, likely John of 1689 was brother to David St
Crawford, David, Sr.	300	David Craford	1677	David Crawford often misspelled with 2 f's i.e. Crafford David Sr.
Croome, Joell -	600			
Crump, Eliz b -	80			
Crump, James -	150			
Crump, Rich d -	60			
Crump, Robt. -	150			
Crump, Stephen -	60	Steph. Crump		
Crump, Wm. 1665	**330**	**Will. Crump**		Crump family early settlers of New Kent
Crutchfield, Jr	400			
Crutchfield, Peter -	400			
Curnell, Andrew -	330			

Name	Acres	Alt. Name	Year	Notes
Dabney, Cornelius **Daboney**	**320**	Mr. Dabbony		Cornelius Dabney I original french spelling = = D'Aubigné Debney, Dabony, Debany, Dabonei, Dabnee, Dabnie, Dabboni, Church Warden in 1684
Daniell, John -	100		1677	**William** Daniel in 1677
Darnell, Rachell -	100			
Davenport, Mea t ?	125			
Davis, Eliazar -	375	Andrew. Davis		
Davis, **John**	80	**John** Davis	1677	**Jeffry** Davis in 1677
Dennett, John -	350			
Depriest, Robt. -	**350**	Rob't Deprosse		*DePriest did not arrive until just before 1689 (was not here for Bacon's Rebellion or signing of the Blissland List of Grievances*
Dibdall, Jn o -	800			
Dodd, John -	300			
Dolerd, Wm. -	50			*?Dillard?*

Name	Acreage	Alt. Name	Year	Notes
Duke, Henry, Esqr. -	325			
Duke, Henry, Esqr. -	170			
Dumas, Jeremiah	**250**			Jerome Dumas was from Poitou-Charentes, France as cited in Baird's Huguenot Emigration to America and The Huguenot, vol. 25 suspect that Dumas/DePriest families were friends prior to Virginia because Dumas was Huguenot who came over with Manakintown group in 1700 but Dumas showing **250a** of land next to DePriest in New Kent in 1704 processioning
Durham, James -	100			
Elderkin, John -	300			
Ellis, Wm. -	100			
Ellison [Ellyson],	520	Rob't Elleson Ellison		
Elmore, Peter -	100			
Elmore, Tho. -	300			
Elmore, Tho., Jun r	100			
England, Wm. -	490			neighbor to DePriest,, widow appeared on 1711 processioning as did Widow DePriest *father = Humphrey?*
English, [Ingles] Mungo -	500			
Eperson, John -	120	Jno. Epecon		*Epperson? Note:* Apperson *recognized Huguenot*
Feare, Edw d -	200			
Fenton, Widdo -	270			
Finch, Edw d -	300			
Fisher, Wm. -	100			
Fleming, Charles wife Susanna	**920**	**Chas. Fleming**	**1677**	**JOHN Fleming in 1677.** Gentry who signed Blisland list of grievances addressed to the King
Forgeson, Wm. -	507			
Foster, Joseph -	800	Capt Joseph Forster		
Francis, Tho. -	150			
Freeman, Wm. -	200			
Gadberry, Tho.	200			
Garland, Edw d -	2600			1734-Inventory of estate of **John** Garland.
Garrat, James -	375	Garrott	1677	JAMES GARRETT in 1677
Gawen, Phillip -	50			

Gentry, Nich o	250	**Mr.** Gentry		
Gibson, Tho. -	370			
Giles, Jn o -	120			
Gill, Nich o -	222	Nic * * *		
Gillmott, Jn o -	160			
Gillmott, Rich d -	150	Rich Gilliam		*? surname match?*
Gills, John -	100			
Glass, Anne -	150			
Glass, Tho. -	**150**		**1677**	**Thomas GLASSE in 1677**
Glassbrook [Glazebrook] Rob t	400			
Gleam, Jn o -	300			
Goodger, Jn o -	200			
Goodring, Alexander -	100			
Gorton, Jn o -	250	John Gontin?		*?surname match?*
Gosling, Wm. -	460			
Graham, Tho. -	250			
Granchaw [*Crenshaw?]* Rob t -	480			
Green, Edw d -	200	**Hen.** Green	1677	**HENRY GREENE in 1677** **oldest = Ralph Green?**
Greenfield, Fran.	80			
Grindge, Rich d	225			

Hairy, John -	280			
Haiselwood, Jn o -	200			
Haiselwood, Tho. -	50			
Handey, Wm -	150			
Hankins, Charles -	340			
Harlow, Tho. -	230			
Harmon, Wm. -	350	Wm. and Rbt Harman	1677	**Robert Harman in 1677.**
[Harrelson], Paul -	360			
Harris, Benj a -	100			
Harris, Edm d -	100	Edward Haris	1677	*Edmund v Edward* **EDWARD HARRISON 1677**
Harris, John -	146			
Harris, Rob t -	75			
Harris, Tho. -	**100**			
Harris, Wm. -	150			
Harris, Wm. -	125			
Harris, Wm. -	100			
Haselwood, Rich d -	100			
Hatfield, Wm. -	218			
Hawes, Haughton distinct surname	850			*Hawes = correct spellling; HAWES store on later map near New Castle*

from :Howe				
Herlock, John -	320			
Hester, Fra -	300	Fran Eastor		Eastor appeared only in 1689, surname = **HESTER**
Hight, John -	100	Jno. Hight		
Hill Jn o -	250			
Hill, Sam ll -	300	**Fran.** Hill		FRAN Hill in 1689, Sam Hill in 1704
Hilton, Jn o -	300			
Hockiday, Wm. -	**300**			Hockaday = correct spelling
Hogg, Jn o, Jun r -	260			
Hogg, Mary -	140			
Hogg, Wm. -	200			
Holdcroft, Henry -	95			
Holled, Sam ll -	100			
Hopkins, Wm. -	200			
Horkeey, John -	800			
Horman, Rob t -	300			
Horsley, Rowland -	**250**	**Rowland Horsley**	**1677**	**Horsley in 1677**
Howes, Job - distinct surname from Hawes	**300**			*Howes, Job*
Howle, Jn o -	150			
Howle, Jn o Jun r -	100			
Huberd, Jn o -	827			
Hughes, Jn o -	**180**	**Bird Hoghes**		Bird presumed to be namesake for Wm Byrd
Hughes, Rees -	400	Rees ?	**1677**	It appears that Rees and Rice were two different people
Hughs, Rob t -	966	Rob't **Hughes**	**1677**	
Hutton, Geo. -	150			

Izard, Fran	**1233**	**Mrs.Isard**		
Jackson, Tho. -	500	Thom. Jackson		
Jarratt, Rob t -	**1600**	**Mr. Jarrott**		
Jeeves, Tho. -	100		**1677**	Thomas GEEVES in 1677
Jenings, Robt. -	100			*Jennings?*
Johnson, Edw d -	150	Edw'd Johnson	**1677**	EDWARD JOHNSON in 1677 Note: 1655 Richard Johnson transported by Mr. Anthony Langston[20]
Johnson, John -	100			
Johnson, Mich ll -	40			
Johnson, Wm. -	265			
		Joanes = Jones? or two different families? Given		Joanes in 1689 Jones in 1704

---

[20] Early Virginia Immigrants by George Cabell Greer

		names don't match up		
Jones, Evan -	500	**Bird** Joanes		*Anthony Jones with 500a in 1620's likely progenitor.*
Jones, Francis -	200	Richard Joanes		
Jones, Fredrick -	500			
Jones, Jane -	200	**Th**os. Joanes		
Jones, John -	100	Jno. Joanes		
Jones, John -	100			
Jones, John -	100			

Keeling, Geo. -	**1500**			*1500a in 1704 but no other mention found*
Kembro [Kimborough?], Jn	540	Jno. Kinborn		
Kembro, Jno, Junr -	150			
King, Eliz b -	**300**	**Rob't King**		

Lacey, Emanuell -	**180**			
Lacey, Tho. -	**100**			
Lacey, Wm. -	**500**			
Lane, Tho. -	100			
Langston				**Langston, John :1681 1300 acres formerly granted to Hannah Clarke and was found to escheat.** **Likely had land <1704 in another County** *Langston/Langdon/Langsdon?* *Laydon = much earlier, not related* *Langston first name = Thomas LangsDON* *first name = John* *Quaker = John Langston*
Laton, Reuben -	100			
Law, James -	100			
Lawson, John -	50			
Lawson, Rich d -	200	**Nichols** Lawsone	**1677**	**NICHOLS LAWSONE in1677**
Leak, Wm. -	280			
Lee, Edw d -	120			
Lesplah, Peter -	100			
Lestrange, Tho. -	200			see also **Alexander** Strange and Henry Strange ("Le" dropped) - became Strainge/Strange
Levermore, Phill -	1000			
Lewis, John -	**375**			
Lewis, John, Esqr. -	**2600**	**Jno. Lewes**		
Lewis, Tho. -	115			
Liddal, Geo. Coll. -	**100**			**Spelling = Lydall**
Lightfoot, John,	**3600**	**Mr. Lightfoot**		

Esqd.				
Linsey, Joseph -	1150			
Linsey, Wm. -	50			
Littlepage, Rich d -	2160	**Mrs.Eliz.** Littlepage		**Francis** LITTLE **in** 1677 Littlepage, Richard grantee (Elizabeth?) only Eliz listed in 1689 Richard Littlepage, his son, succeeded to his property at his death, April 20, 1688. Richard Littlepage, JR. married Frances Austin. He died March 20, 1717, and his wife survived him until 1732 Sheriff of New Kent 1705 M' Richard Littlepage deceased ye 20th day of April 1688. (Sr) Richard Littlepage Gen' Departed this Life March ye 20, 1717. (Jr)
Lochester, Edw d -	80			
Lochester, Robt. -	80			
Logwood, Tho. -	100		**1677**	THOMAS **LOWNELL in 1677?**
Lovell, Charles	**250**	**Chas. Lovell**	**1677**	**Charles LOVALLi n 1677**
Lovell, Geo. -	**920**			
Luke, Jn o -	150			

Mackeny, Eliz	250			
Madox, John -	300			
Mage, Peter -	450			
Major, Wm.	456	Wm. Major		
Markham, Tho. -	100			
Marr, Geo. -	100			
Martin, James -	**100**	**Hen. Martin**		*Henry & Thomas- from different Martin than John Martin*
Martin, John -	**300**			
Martin, Martin	**150**	**Martin Martin**		
Martin, Tho. -	**100**	**Thos. Martin**		
Martin, Wm. -	**230**	**Wm. Martinn**		
Masey [Massie] Peter -	100		**1677**	**Massey, Peter:** **Later Thomas Massey =**
Mask, Jn o -	411	Jno Mark?		
Matray, Tho. -	382	Jno. Mashay?		
Mattlow, James -	150			
McKgehe, Wm. -	131 ½ 1/			*Odd acreage amount - was the normal plot size of a Manakintown Huguenot Could be " MaGeeHee" is French misspelling,, not Scottish*
McKing, Alexander -	170			
McKoy, Jn o – Macoy	**300**		**1677**	*MACOY spelled several different ways*
Meacon [Macon],	**270**	**Gideon MACON**		Macon!

Gideon - *wife =Martha Woodward*				
Meanley, Wm. -	100	Wm. Meanly		
Medlock, John -	350			
Mellington, Wm. Jun r -	450			
Melton, Rich d -	290			
Merfield, John -	210			
Merideth, James -	270			
Merridith, Geo. -	400			
Merriweather, Nich o -	**3327**			
Michell, Tho. -	300			
Millington, Wm.	**200**	**Wm. Millington**	**1677**	**Martin Middlton in 1677**
Mills, Nich o	300	Nic. Mills		Precinct Neighbor to DePriest
Minis, Tho. - MIMS	200		*1677*	**THOMAS MIMS in 1677** *Thomas Mims, owned 750a in Henrico and 200a in New Kent On Dec 23, 1714, Thomas Mims received a patent for 500 acres on the south side of the main branch of Tuckahoe Creek in Henrico County, paying 50 shillings. 3 years later, In Aug 1717, Thomas Mims "of Henrico Co, planter" sold a portion of this property,*
Mitchell, Stephen, Jun r	200	Steph. Mitchell		
Mitchell, Stephen, Jun r	75			
Mitchell, Wm. -	512	Mr. Mitchell		
Mohan [Mohun] Warwick -	850			
Moon, Stephen	70	Steph. Moon		
Moor, Anne -	75	**James** Moor	**1677**	**JAMES** Moore in 1677
Moor, Edw d -	65			
Moor, Jn o -	250			
Moor, Pelham -	125	Pelham Moore		
Moor, Tho. -	65		1677	*THOMAS MOOREMAN in 1677?*
Morgan, Edw d -	50	Edw. Morgan	1677	**EDWARD MORGAN in** 1677
Morgan, Matthew -	210			
Morreigh, John -	100			
Morris, John -	450	**Lyon** Moriss		*LYON is location in France Morris = Frencl*
Morris, Rob t -	245	**Lyon** Morriss		**Nicolaus Morris = qualified Huguenot** related? likely French father naming child first name "Lyon" in 1689
Moss, James -	720	Mr. James Moss		
Moss, Sam ll -	200	**Geo. Moss**	1677?	**WILL: MOSSE 1677?**
Moss, Tho. -	430	Thom. Moss		
Moxon, Wm. -	100			

Murroho, Jn o -	100			
Neaves, James -	150			
Nonia, Rich d -	100			
Norris, Wm. -	100			
Nucholl, James -	**300**	**Thom Nichols**	**1677**	**l**
Osling, John -	150	Jno. Osling		
Otey, John -	290			
Oudton, Matt. -	190			
Page, John, **Jun r -**	400			
Page, Mary Mad'm -	3450	Capt.& Col'l **Page**	1677	**THOMAS PAGE 1677** **Col'l John wife Alice Lucken, Susana Page**
Paite [Pate] Jerim[iah]	220			
Paite [Pate], John -	1500			
Par, John -	200	Jno. Parks		
Park, Coll [Daniel] -	**7000**			
Park, Jn o Jun r -	300	Jno. Park s		
Pasley, **Robt. -**	300	**Mr. Wm** Pasley/ Jno. Parks		
?	300	Thos. Paddison		? died between1689 and 1704?
Pease, John -	100	Jno. Peard		
[Poindexter] Pendexter, Geo	**1490**			
Pendexter [Poindexter], Tho	**1000**	**Mr.** Poindexter		
Penix, Edw d -	200	**Dow.** Penix		1689 Dow (widow of xx, 1704 Edw (son?)
Perkins, John -	120			
Perkins, Wm. -	305			
Petever, Tho. -	100			
Petty, John -	**2190**			
Petty, Stephen -	200			
Philip, Geo. -	100			
Pickley, Tho. -	281			
Pittlader, Tho. -	295			
Pittlader, Wm. -	147			
Plantine, Peter -	240			
Porter, John -	100			
Pullam [Pulliam], Wm.	**575**			
Purdy, Nich o -	200			
Purly, John -	100			
Pyraul, James -	150			

Raglin [Ragland], Evan	300	Edw'd Ragglin	
Raglin [Ragland], Evan jun r -	100		
Raglin [ragland], Tho. -	100		
Randolph, Widd o	100		*It is very curious that a Randolph would only have 100a which typically indicates and "EX indentured servant". Though many of the Virginian Randolphs were wealthy, it is possible that this Widow Randolph was not part of that wealthy clan and might well have been the mother of Elizabeth, first wife of Robert DePriest, whose son **Guillaume named his first son "Randolph"** possible to honor his mother (Elizabeth) who died shortly after Guillaume's birth AND to <u>imply</u> family connection to the wealthy Randolphs*
Raymond, James -	80		
Redwood, John -	1078		
Reyley, Jno. -	100	Jno. Realy	
Reynold, Tho. -	355	Tho. Ronalle (had daughter named Judith b. 1688)	Tho. **Renalls** in the Christ Church Parish, Virginia Records, 1653-1812 Primary Name:Jno Relation:son Parent 1:Tho. Renalls Baptism date:18 Feb 1684 ***Reynold, Tho. -355. Tho. Ronalle:1689 Same person?*** Acreage 355 vs. DePriest at 350 (same social class) Reynold / Ronalle / Renall = French Possible father of Judith who married Guillaume DePriest Listed as recognized Huguenot is Reneau / Reynaud / Reno (Louis de) **Renall, Reynolds** *John Reynolds was murdered in 1696* Fryday y⁰ 30ᵗʰ of October 1696 Anne Grey of Blisland Parish in New Kent County convicted and condemned for yᵉ murder of John Reynolds, presenting a petition sign'd by many of the principal Inhabitants of this Colony praying a repreive for her, & being rep'sented to his Excellency by yᵉ Councill as an object of mercy his Exᶜʸ granted her a repreive till the fourth day of October Genᶫˡ Court next that in the mean time she may apply for his Maᵗ Grace and pardon.[106]
Reynolds, Jonah -	50	Joanes Ronalls.	First name - Jonas, Jonah, Joanes?
Reynolds, Sam ll -	820		
Rhoads [Rodes],	175		

Charles -				
Rice, Tho. -	300			
Richard, Eman -	1250			
Richardson, Henry -	300			
Richardson, John -	1450			
Richardson, Richard -	890			
Ross, Wm. -	150			
Round Tree [Roundtree], Wm	100			
Rule, Widdo. -	50			
Russell, John -	550			
Salmon, Thomas -	**50**			
Sanders, James -	60	James Sanders		
Sanders, John -	130	James Sanders		
Sanders, Tho. -	25			
Sanders, Wm. -	40			
Sandidge, Jn o -	100			
Scott, John -	300			
Scrugg, Jn o -	50			
Scrugg, Rich d -	100			
Sexton, Wm -	80			
Shears, Paul -	200			
Sherriff, Henry -	100			
Sims, John -	**1000**			
Slater, James -	700			
Smith, James -	80			
Smith, Nath ll -	82			
Smith, **Roger** -	300	**Mr. Geo.Smith.**	**1677**	**GEO SMITH in 1677,** *Roger = son???*
Smith, **Wm.** -	110			
Snead, John	75	**John Snead**	**1677**	**Henry** Sneed in 1677 Henry **son to Jn" Snead** bap' ye 8th day of May **1687,** William son to John Snead bap' ye 9 of Novem", 1690.\\ *Note: Sarah Snead daughter of John Snead married John DePriest son of Robert DePriest*
Snead, Tho. -	200	**Thos. Snead**		
Spear, Robt. -	450	Rob't Speare	**1677**	**ROBERT SPEARE in 1677**
Sprattlin, Andrew -	654		**1677**	**ANDREW SPRAGLINGE in1677**
Stamp, Ralph -	625			
Stanley, Tho. -	150			
Stanup [Stanhope], Capt. [John] -	1024			
Stanup [Stanhope], Rich d	325			

Name	Acres		Year	Notes
Stephens, Wm. -	100			
Stepping, Tho. -	350			
Strange, Alexander *1 Benjamin > Alexander,Sr >Alexxander Jr. Henry = ? brother to Benjamin?	**450**	**Elex. Strange**	1677	**HENRY STRANGE** in 1677
Styles, John -	200			
Sunter, Stephen -	478			
Symons, George -	125			
Symons, Josiah -	100			

Name	Acres		Year	Notes
Tapp, Jn o -	110			
Tate, James -	160	James Tate		An daug' to James Tate bap' ye 29 of August 1689. Mary daut" of James Tate baptized the 20 April 1694 Robt Tate 1728:
Taylor, Joseph -	150			
Taylor, Lemuell -	212			
Taylor, Tho. -	25			
	350	Tho. Taylor		
Terrell, Wm. -	400		**1677**	RICHMOND TERRELL in 1677 *TERRY and Terrell are 2 different surnames*
Thomasse's Orphans -	500	Sam. Thomas		
Thompson, Capt. -	**2600**	Rob't Thomson		
Thompson, James -	100			
Thorp, Tho. -	200			
Thurmond [Thurman] Rich d -	131 1/2			ACCERAGE = amount allocated to a Huguenot in Manakintown
Tinsley, Cornelius -	220			
Tinsley, Jn o -	130			
Tinsley, Tho. -	**150**	**Thos. *TINSLEY* Tinsly**	1677	**Tinsley in 1677** Thomas Tinsley, of Totopotomoy Creek Thomas arrived in Jamestown, Virginia Colony, in 1638, his transportation furnished by John Robins of James City County. His will is dated October 9, 1700, New Kent County, Virginia. Witnesses were Richard Meriwether, Jeremiah Pope, and John Oaks. It was recorded in 1702, in New Kent County, upon the corporal oaths of Nicholas Meriwether and John Oaks.
Tony, Alexander -	**170**			Progenitor of the Toney family. Wm DePriest, the counterfeiter, married Tabitha Toney daughter of Charles Toney
Tovis, Edm d -	100			

Town, Eliz b -	100			
Tucker, Tho -	700			
Tully, Wm. TALLEY	**200**	Jno. **Talle = Talley**		
Turn'r, Wm. -	250	Wm. Turner		*Vestry Clerk as was **Henry** Turner*
Turner, Geo. -	400			
Turner, Geo. Jun r -	200			
Turner, Henry -	250	Hen. Turner	**1677**	**HENRY TURNER in 1677** **served as Vestry Clerk**
Turner, James -	50			
Twitty, Thomas -	200			
Tyler -	100			
Tyrey [Tyree?], Thom. -	190			
Tyrrey, Alexand r -	210			
Tyrrey, James -	150			

Upsherd, Jo n -	60			
Vaughan, John -	**250**	**John Vaughn**	**1677**	**JOHN VAUGHAN in 1677** **Jn" Vaughan and Sara Poindexter** **(Huguenot) married ye 5th day of No-** **vem", 16S6.**
Vaughan, Vincent -	410			
Vaughan, Wm. -	300			
Venables [Venable], Abr: -	100	Abra. Venable		
Venables [Venable], John -	200			
Vice, Amer. -	**50**			**HUGUENOT!**

Waddill, Jn o -	40	Jno. Waddell	**1677**	**JOHN WADELL in 1677** **also, Waddill** **John & Wm Waddel vs Samuel Waddy**
Waddill, Wm. -	375			
Waddy, Sam ll -	150	Sam'l Waddy		
Waid [Wade], James -	150			
Walker, Capt. -	400			
Walker, Wm. -	650			
Walton, Edw d -	**450**	**Dow Wallton**	**1677**	**EDWARD WALTON in 1677**
Walton, Edw d -	150			
Warring, Peter -	88			
Watkins, Wm. -	50			
Watson, Theophilus	325	Thos. Wattson		
Weaver, Sam -	**100**	**Sam'l Weaver**		**Early Huguenot surname in New Kent!** *Descendent of Samuel Weaver who* *survived 1622 Indian massacre?*
Webb, Mary -	200			
Webster, Joseph -	80			
West, Giles -	200			
West, Nath. -	**6370**			

Wharton, Tho. -	270		
Wheeler, John -	75		
White, Jno -	320		
White, John -	190		
Wilkes, Joseph -	250		
Willford, Charles -	100		
Williams, Clerk -	300	**Widow Williams**	1677	**WILLIAM LEWIS 1677**
Williams, Tho. -	100		
Williams, Wm. -	**100**			*Alias name used by Wm DePriest, counterfeiter*
Willis, Fran. -	134		
Willis, Stephen -	500		
Wilmore, Jno -	100		
Wilso, James -	60		
Wilson, John -	200		
Winfry, **Charles** -	100		1677	?HENRY WINIFRIDE in1677
Wingfield, Tho. -	150		
Winstone, Antho. -	310		
Winstone, Isaac -	850	**Wm.** Winston	
Winstone, Sarah -	275		
Wintby, Jacob -	250		
Wood, Henry -	100		
Wood, Walter -	100		
Woodall, James -	200		
Woodson, John -	600		
Woody, James -	130	James Woody	
Woody, John -	100		
Woody, Symon -	50		
Worrin, Robt. -	300		
Wyatt, Alice -	1300	Mr. Hen. **Wyatt**	
Yeoell, **Judith** -	150			*Judith = widow or spinster*
Yeoman, John -	50		

Observations From Comparison of Lists of Landowners for Different Dates:

- A few New Kent Blisland Rebels from 1677 remained in New Kent in 1704. Quit Rents of landowners.
- Virginians typically made several moves before settling. Later lists of processioning beyond 1704 show many names in 1704 no longer in St. Paul's parish (indicating death or simply moving on to "greener pastures").
- Some landowner surnames in the 1689 processioning are still there in the 1704 processioning but with different given names, likely indicating that the **father died and the son** inherited the land, e.g.:

Aimy's version after digesting the above data from "The Book."

By analyzing land ownership in Colonial Virginia through such detailed comparison tables, you can uncover a variety of insights:

Surname Evolution and Stability

1. *Surname Spelling Variations:*
   - *Comparing the different spellings of surnames over time (e.g., "Renall Allen" in 1689 versus "Reynold Allen" in 1704) helps track families and understand the evolution of surname spellings. This can indicate phonetic changes, transcription errors, or regional dialect influences.*

2. *Name Consistency:*
   - *Families with consistent surname spellings across different records (e.g., "Bassett" consistently spelled the same in 1677, 1689, and 1704) suggest strong lineage continuity and potentially higher social standing or literacy, leading to more standardized records.*

Land Ownership and Economic Status

3. *Land Accumulation:*
   - *By comparing acreage over time, one can identify families that expanded their holdings (e.g., "Wm. Bassett" with significant acreage increase from 550 acres in 1704 to additional landholdings), indicating wealth accumulation and potentially increased social or political influence.*

4. *New Landowners:*
   - *Highlighting new landowners in 1704, as shown by gray shading, reveals immigration patterns, economic mobility, and the growth of the colonial*

population. It can show who benefited from land redistribution or economic opportunities post-Bacon's Rebellion.

Social and Political Involvement

5. **Rebellion Participants:**
   - Identifying landowners who signed the 1677 Blissland grievances (e.g., "Rob't Anderson") shows their involvement in political activities, such as dissent against the Crown following Bacon's Rebellion. This can indicate their political affiliations and potential conflicts with colonial authorities.

6. **Community Leadership:**
   - Families repeatedly appearing in records (e.g., the "Harris" family) might have played significant roles in the community, serving as local leaders, church wardens, or other positions of influence. This can be inferred from consistent landholdings and participation in local governance, as seen with "Cornelius Dabney," a church warden in 1684.

Demographic and Genealogical Trends

7. **Family Continuity and Connections:**
   - Observing family names across generations (e.g., "Anderson" family with multiple entries) helps build genealogical profiles and track family migration and expansion within the colony. This continuity suggests stable family

Parish processioning records are valuable tools for genealogists researching land ownership in colonial Virginia. These records were created as part of the Anglican

Church's process of periodically walking and marking the boundaries of parish lands. Here is an example of how to use these records to identify land owned by an individual:

Example: Using Parish Processioning Records

Context

Let's say you are researching an ancestor named John Smith who lived in Hanover County, Virginia, in the mid-18th century. You have reason to believe he owned land there, but you must pinpoint its location.

Step-by-Step Process

1. *Locate Parish Processioning Records:*
   - *Parish processioning records can often be found in county court records, parish vestry books, or specific collections of colonial records. For Hanover County, you might consult the vestry book of St. Paul's Parish, which covered that area.*

2. *Examine the Records:*
   - *Look for entries that mention John Smith. Processioning records usually list the names of landowners whose property boundaries were walked and confirmed.*

3. *Interpret the Records:*
   - *An entry might read something like: "In the year 1750, the land of John Smith was processioned. The boundaries were found to be as follows: beginning at the large oak tree at the corner of John Davis's land, thence north along the creek to the stone marker by William Johnson's field..."*
   - *This description provides key boundary markers and neighboring landowners.*

4. *Cross-Reference with Other Records:*

o   *Use land grants, deeds, and plats to cross-reference the details found in the processioning records. For example, if John Smith's land was described in a deed as "bounded by John Davis to the south and William Johnson to the north," it confirms the processioning record.*

5.   *Map the Land:*

o   *Using the boundary descriptions, create a map of John Smith's land. Modern mapping tools, historical maps, and GIS (Geographic Information Systems) can help visualize the property.*

Sample Entry and Interpretation

Vestry Book of St. Paul's Parish, Hanover County, 1750:

"The lands of John Smith, John Davis, William Johnson, and others in the lower precinct were processioned. The processioning party, consisting of William Harris, John Thompson, and Robert Carter, reported the boundaries as follows: starting from the large oak at John Davis's corner, following the creek north to the stone marker at William Johnson's field, then east to the pine tree near the old road, and south back to the starting oak tree."

Interpretation:

- *Large Oak Tree: Southern boundary, shared with John Davis.*
- *Creek: Natural boundary forming the northern edge.*
- *Stone Marker: Indicates a fixed boundary point on the northern side near William Johnson's field.*
- *Pine Tree Near Old Road: Eastern boundary marker.*
- *Back to Starting Oak: Completes the boundary loop.*

Cross-Reference:

- ***Deed Reference***: A 1748 deed mentions John Smith's property as "beginning at John Davis's oak, running north along the creek to William Johnson's stone marker, east to the pine near the road, and back south to the oak."
- ***Land Grant***: An earlier land grant in 1735 describes a similar boundary, confirming long-term ownership and consistent boundary lines.

Mapping:

- Create a map using the described boundaries:
  - Mark the large oak at the southwest corner.
  - Follow the creek north to the stone marker.
  - Extend east to the pine tree.
  - Return south to the starting oak.

Conclusion

Parish processioning records, when combined with other land records, can provide a detailed picture of land ownership and boundaries. This process helps genealogists identify and map ancestral properties, offering valuable insights into the lives and locations of early Virginia settlers.

AI for Genealogists as of July 2024

Note: AI is snowballing and will predictably increase its "learning" daily, so I have chosen to show the date of this work, knowing that different people may be given different results in the future.

Prompt: What genealogy apps already use AI?

ChatCPT-3.5 as of 06/24/2024

Several genealogy apps incorporate AI (Artificial Intelligence) to enhance their features and provide users with advanced capabilities. Here are some genealogy apps that already use AI:

1. *Ancestry.com:*

   - *Ancestry.com utilizes AI algorithms for record matching, DNA analysis, intelligent search, and personalized recommendations. AI helps users discover historical records, find potential relatives, and build comprehensive family trees.*

2. *MyHeritage:*

   - *MyHeritage integrates AI technologies for features like Smart Matches, which automatically identify matches between user-contributed family trees and historical records. It also offers DNA testing services with AI-driven ethnicity estimates and DNA matches.*

3. *FamilySearch:*

   - *FamilySearch uses AI for record matching and indexing, making historical records more accessible to users. AI algorithms help users connect with their ancestors by suggesting potential matches and providing hints for further research.*

4. *Findmypast:*

   o *Findmypast employs AI for record matching and search optimization. It helps users uncover historical documents and connect with relatives through smart matching algorithms powered by AI technologies.*

5. *Living DNA:*

   o *Living DNA uses AI for ethnicity estimation based on DNA data provided by users. It analyzes genetic markers to provide detailed ethnicity reports and ancestry insights.*

6. *23andMe:*

   o *While primarily focused on genetic testing, 23andMe incorporates AI for ancestry composition analysis, genetic health risk assessments, and DNA matching with relatives. AI algorithms help users understand their genetic heritage and health predispositions.*

7. *Geni:*

   o *Geni utilizes AI for collaborative family tree building, suggesting potential relatives and helping users merge duplicate profiles. It also offers DNA testing services with AI-driven ancestry reports.*

These genealogy apps leverage AI technologies to automate tasks, improve data accuracy, provide personalized insights, and enhance the overall user experience in exploring family history and ancestry

Prompt: How Does Ancestry.com Use AI

ChatCPT-3.5 as of 06/24/2024

Ancestry.com incorporates AI (Artificial Intelligence) in various aspects of its services to enhance

genealogical research and provide personalized experiences for users. Here are some key ways Ancestry.com utilizes AI:

1. *Record Matching and Indexing:*
   - Ancestry.com uses AI algorithms to match user-provided family tree data with historical records such as census records, birth/death certificates, immigration records, and military documents.
   - AI helps in automating the process of indexing and digitizing these records, making it easier for users to find relevant information about their ancestors.

2. *DNA Analysis and Ethnicity Estimation:*
   - AI is employed to analyze DNA data from users who opt for DNA testing kits. This analysis includes identifying genetic markers associated with specific regions or ethnicities.
   - Ancestry.com uses AI to provide ethnicity estimates to users based on their DNA data and to match them with potential genetic relatives within the Ancestry.com database.

3. *Smart Search and Recommendations:*
   - Ancestry.com's search functionality is powered by AI algorithms that help users find relevant historical records, family connections, and potential ancestors.
   - AI also provides personalized recommendations to users based on their family tree data, search history, and genetic information, helping them discover new branches of their family tree.

4. *Machine Learning for Family Tree Building:*
   - Machine learning techniques are utilized to assist users in building and expanding their family trees. AI algorithms analyze existing family tree data to suggest potential relatives or missing connections.
   - Ancestry.com's AI systems provide hints and suggestions for further research, making the process of building a comprehensive family tree more efficient and accurate.

5. *Historical Insights and Contextual Information:*

  o *AI is used to analyze historical context and provide insights into historical events, migration patterns, and social trends relevant to users' family histories.*

  o *This contextual information enhances users' understanding of their ancestors' lives within the broader historical context, making the genealogical research experience more meaningful.*

Overall, Ancestry.com leverages AI technologies to streamline genealogical research, improve record matching accuracy, provide DNA-based insights, offer personalized recommendations, and enrich users' understanding of their family history.

Can AI do graphics?

PROMPT: What about creating graphics for Genealogy

ChatCPT-3.5 as of 06/24/2024 (free version does not include graphics)

Note: Chat 4.0 and higher (involves a fee) can create graphics directly from the Chat GPT Prompt without going to a dedicated AI application for creating graphics i.e, **DALL-E by OpenAI** *is included in Chat GPT 4.0 or higher)*

Yes, AI can be used to create graphics for genealogy. There are several ways AI can assist in this process:

1. **Automatic Family Tree Generation:** *AI algorithms can analyze genealogical data and automatically generate family tree diagrams, including relationships, dates, and names of ancestors and descendants.*

2. **Enhanced Image Restoration:** *AI can help restore old or damaged family photos by removing noise, enhancing clarity, and adding missing details, making them suitable for use in genealogy presentations or albums.*

3. **Data Visualization:** *AI-powered tools can create visualizations such as timelines, geographical maps showing ancestral migration patterns, and charts depicting demographic data related to family history.*

4. *Customized Design Templates:* AI can generate customized design templates for family history books, posters, or digital presentations, incorporating genealogical data into visually appealing layouts.

5. *Facial Recognition and Ancestry Analysis:* AI can analyze facial features in photos to identify ancestors and provide insights into genetic ancestry, helping users visualize their heritage.

By leveraging AI capabilities, genealogists can enhance their research presentations, share family histories more effectively, and preserve ancestral memories through visually engaging graphics.

PROMPT: What are some AI applications that can generate illustrations, line art, etc? ChatGPT-3.5 as of 06/25/2024

Several AI applications and tools can generate illustrations, line art, and other forms of digital art. Here are some notable ones:

1. *DALL-E by OpenAI (Included in Chat GPT 4.0 or higher)*

- *Description*: DALL-E is an AI model developed by OpenAI that can generate images from textual descriptions.
- *Use Case*: You can describe an image or scene in text, and DALL-E will create a corresponding illustration.

2. *DeepArt.io*

- *Description*: DeepArt.io uses neural networks to turn photos into artwork inspired by various artistic styles.
- *Use Case*: Upload a photo, select an art style, and the tool will generate an artistic rendition of the original image.

3. *Artbreeder*

- *Description*: Artbreeder allows users to create and modify images of faces, landscapes, and other subjects using AI.
- *Use Case*: Combine and edit images to generate new, unique illustrations.

4. AutoDraw

- *Description*: AutoDraw is an AI experiment by Google that turns sketches into professional drawings.
- *Use Case*: Sketch something rough, and AutoDraw will suggest and refine the drawing into a more polished version.

5. PaintsChainer

- *Description*: PaintsChainer is an AI-based tool that colorizes line art.
- *Use Case*: Upload line art, and the tool will automatically apply colors based on different styles and preferences.

6. Deep Dream Generator

- *Description*: This tool uses a neural network called Deep Dream to transform images into dream-like visuals.
- *Use Case*: Generate surreal and artistic versions of your images by applying different Deep Dream settings.

7. NVIDIA GauGAN

- *Description*: GauGAN is an AI tool by NVIDIA that converts rough sketches into photorealistic images.
- *Use Case*: Draw simple shapes and lines, and GauGAN will turn them into realistic scenes with appropriate textures and details.

8. Runway ML

- *Description*: Runway ML offers various AI models for creative tasks, including generating illustrations and animations.
- *Use Case*: Use pre-trained models to create digital art, animations, and other visual content.

9. *ToonMe*

- *Description*: ToonMe is an app that uses AI to transform photos into cartoon or comic-style images.
- *Use Case*: Upload a photo, and the app will generate a cartoon version with different styles.

10. *AI Painter (DeepArt)*

- *Description*: AI Painter uses deep learning to convert images into artworks inspired by famous artists.
- *Use Case*: Upload an image, choose an artistic style, and the tool will create a painting-like version of the image.

These AI tools provide a range of options for generating illustrations, line art, and other forms of digital art, making it easier for artists and non-artists alike to create visually compelling content.

Note: I declared that NO AI was used to create "The Book," so I had limited options for using graphics.

However, below are some AI-generated illustrations I created using various Graphic AI tools to show how rich the visuals could be to show the contrast of the social classes of the Gentry and Yeoman:

AI May Not Answer All Your Questions, But…

ChatGPT is pre-trained on vast amounts of data but needs to delve deeper into specific facts on highly specialized subjects like genealogy. However, it can still assist in making your research efforts more focused and effective.

Example   - I entered the following particular prompt looking for names:

ChatCPT-3.5 as of 06/24/2024

I need access to real-time data or specific historical records such as the 1704 Virginia quit rents. However, I can provide general information about land ownership trends during that period.

In the early 18th century, land ownership in Virginia was concentrated among wealthy landowners, including prominent families such as the Washingtons, Jeffersons, and Randolphs. These families often acquired extensive land holdings through grants, purchases, or inheritance. Plantation owners, particularly those in tobacco cultivation, typically held substantial acreage.

Suppose you need specific information about land acquisitions exceeding 1000 acres in the 1704 Virginia quit rents. In that case, I recommend consulting historical archives, libraries, or online repositories specializing in colonial land records and property ownership in Virginia during that era.

ChatCPT-3.5 as of 06/24/2024

Here are some of the best sources for data about people in 17th-century Virginia:

1. **Library of Virginia:** *The Library of Virginia is an excellent resource for historical documents, including census records, land patents, court records, wills, and colonial-era manuscripts.*

2. ***Virginia Historical Society:*** *The Virginia Historical Society (now known as the Virginia Museum of History & Culture) maintains a vast collection of primary sources related to Virginia's history, including genealogical records, diaries, letters, and artifacts.*

3. ***Colonial Records of Virginia:*** *The colonial records of Virginia, including the "Virginia Colonial Abstracts" series and the "Journals of the House of Burgesses of Virginia," provide valuable insights into the lives of early settlers, landowners, and government proceedings.*

4. ***FamilySearch:*** *FamilySearch, operated by The Church of Jesus Christ of Latter-day Saints, offers a wealth of genealogical records and historical documents, including birth and death records, marriage registers, probate records, and immigration records related to Virginia settlers.*

5. ***Historical Societies and Museums:*** *Local historical societies, museums, and heritage organizations in Virginia often have archives and collections that contain information about early settlers, families, and communities in the 17th century.*

6. ***Online Archives and Databases:*** *Digital archives such as Early American Imprints, Early American Newspapers, and Colonial Williamsburg's Digital Library provide access to digitized primary sources, newspapers, maps, and historical documents relevant to Virginia's colonial history.*

7. ***University Libraries:*** *University libraries with strong history departments, such as the University of Virginia Library and the College of William & Mary Libraries, offer extensive collections of manuscripts, rare books, maps, and archival materials pertaining to early Virginia history.*

By exploring these sources, researchers and genealogists can uncover valuable data about the people, families, and communities of 17th-century Virginia, enriching our understanding of colonial life and society in the region.

This book primarily used the free version of ChatGPT as detailed below (i.e., ChatGPT-3.5)

Free (as of July 2024)	Upgrade to Plus
Assistance with writing, problem solving and more Access to GPT-3.5 Limited access to GPT-4o Limited access to advanced data analysis, file uploads, vision, web browsing, and custom GPTs	Early access to new features Access to GPT-4, GPT-4o, GPT-3.5 Up to 5x more messages for GPT-4o Access to advanced data analysis, file uploads, vision, and web browsing DALL·E image generation Create and use custom GPTs

PROMPT: What Are The Major Differences Of Using Chatgpt-3.5 And Chatgpt-4.0 For Genealogy

ChatGPT-4.0 as of 06/26/2024

Using ChatGPT-3.5 versus ChatGPT-4.0 for genealogy research can present several notable differences, largely due to improvements in language understanding, contextual awareness, and handling complex queries that were integrated into the newer model. Here's a breakdown of some of the major differences:

Improved Contextual Understanding:

ChatGPT-3.5: *While capable of handling a range of queries, it might struggle with highly contextual or nuanced questions that require understanding subtle differences in genealogical terms or historical contexts.*

ChatGPT-4.0: Enhanced to better grasp the context and nuances of user inquiries, making it more effective in understanding complex genealogical and historical queries. This includes better disambiguation of similar names, places, and events across different time periods.

Handling of Complex Queries:

ChatGPT-3.5: Might require more specific prompts to generate detailed responses or follow-up with multiple questions to narrow down the scope of the inquiry.

ChatGPT-4.0: Improved ability to manage and respond to complex queries in one go, providing more comprehensive and detailed answers that can combine multiple elements (like dates, relationships, and places) more effectively.

Accuracy and Detail in Responses:

ChatGPT-3.5: Generally reliable, but may occasionally produce responses that require verification or lack depth in technical subjects such as genealogical records or specific historical events.

ChatGPT-4.0: Offers enhanced accuracy and a deeper level of detail, beneficial for genealogy enthusiasts who need precise information about lineage, historical records, or ancestral backgrounds.

Training Data and Knowledge Base:

Both versions are trained up to a certain cut-off date (September 2021 for GPT-3.5 and January 2022 for GPT-4.0), but ChatGPT-4.0 includes training on a more diverse set of data sources, potentially offering broader insights and understanding in responses related to historical and genealogical research.

User Interaction and Error Handling:

ChatGPT-3.5: Might not handle misunderstandings or incorrect information as smoothly, requiring more input from the user to correct course.

ChatGPT-4.0: Better at detecting and correcting errors in the interaction, providing clarifications, and guiding the conversation back on track if it detects confusion or misinterpretation.

Integration and Application:
ChatGPT-4.0: With its advanced capabilities, it might integrate more seamlessly with other tools and databases for genealogy, offering a more user-friendly experience for researchers who use AI to complement traditional genealogical methods.

For genealogists, the improvements in ChatGPT-4.0 could translate into more effective research sessions, where they can quickly get accurate historical contexts, decipher old records, or understand complex family relationships with less effort and more confidence in the information provided.

The following was added on 5/1/2025 after the original publish date of 6/27/2024

Using Chat GPT to inquire about AI - Sample Prompt and response:

You said: Explain how AI should be considered as an always available expert.

ChatGPT said:

Certainly. Here's a clear and thoughtful explanation of how **AI should be considered as an "always-available expert"**—especially useful for publications, toolkits, or education materials:

☐ AI as an Always-Available Expert

What it means, and how to use it wisely

Artificial Intelligence—like ChatGPT—is best understood not as a "robot brain," but as an **on-demand, expert-level assistant** that never sleeps, never gets tired, and can help make sense of almost anything.

Think of it as a **team of thousands of experts**, compressed into one voice, ready whenever you are.

☐ What Makes AI Expert-Like?

- **Trained on massive amounts of information**
  AI has read millions of books, articles, studies, and public datasets. It can cross-reference patterns and summarize data far faster than any human could.
- **Instant synthesis and recall**
  Ask a question, and it draws from its vast memory to generate a concise, coherent, and context-aware answer in seconds.
- **Multilingual, multi-disciplinary, and unbiased by fatigue**
  Whether it's law, medicine, psychology, philosophy, politics, or tech—AI doesn't need to "look something up." It processes across fields in real time.

- **No appointments, no wait times, no time zones.**
  Whether it's 3 p.m. or 3 a.m., AI is ready. This makes it ideal for late-night research, quick decisions, or clarifying something before a meeting or conversation.
- **Scalable assistance**
  It can generate outlines, improve writing, break down complex topics, or simulate different perspectives—instantly and simultaneously

How to Use AI Effectively as an Expert Assistant

Goal	Example Prompt
Learn something new	"Explain blockchain in simple terms."
Refine your message	"Help me reword this for clarity and empathy."
Prepare for debate	"Give me talking points both for and against this idea."
Break down complexity	"Summarize this legal opinion in plain English."
Analyze data or patterns	"What are the economic trends in X region?"
Solve creative blocks	"Generate 5 new ways to frame this article."

But Remember: Expert ≠ All-Knowing

- **AI doesn't have lived experience or emotions.**
- **It can reflect bias from its training data.**
- **It doesn't "know" truth—it models likely answers.**
- **It needs you to verify important or sensitive information.**

The smartest use of AI is not to surrender your judgment—but to sharpen it.

AI is your always-available expert—not to replace human wisdom, but to elevate it.

When used with intention, it becomes your personal think tank, writing coach, research assistant, and brainstorming partner—all in one.

AI is your always-available expert—not to replace human wisdom, but to elevate it.